ODYSSEY

OF A

SCIENTIST

ODYSSEY
OF A
SCIENTIST

An Autobiography

Hans Kalmus
AND DAVID BENEDICTUS

Weidenfeld and Nicolson
London

George Weidenfeld and Nicolson Ltd
91 Clapham High Street, London SW4 7TA

ISBN 0 297 82077 X

Typeset at The Spartan Press Ltd, Lymington, Hants
Printed in Great Britain by Butler & Tanner Ltd,
Frome & London

Contents

Foreword

When I was first approached by Professor Hans Kalmus to help him organise the autobiography, on which he had been working for so many years, he explained to me that, as a biologist, he anticipated that at the most he had just five years to live, which was why he had begun to feel a little more urgent about the completion of this book. He wanted it to be both interesting to the general public, who had bought his book, *Genetics*, in such gratifying quantities, and useful to the young scientist, who might learn from Kalmus's life and academic history the direction which his own career should take. I little thought, at that first cordial meeting in Harpenden, that the five years would be so savagely reduced. Within a few months Hans had died – very suddenly and peacefully – and his family was faced with the dilemma of whether or not to proceed with the book. I hoped they would agree that I should complete it, and they did.

Initially Hans and I sat with a tape recorder in his sunny living room, and, when we had worked our way through two or three hours of reminiscences, we would break for lunch and Nussy, his wife, would regale us with some of the finest cooking I have ever enjoyed. As I finished printing out Chapter 1 and Chapter 2, in an especially large font so he would be able to read it despite his failing eyesight, I sent them to Hans, and he returned them to me with many emendations and notes in his spidery and almost entirely illegible handwriting. I was able to incorporate these changes into the first two chapters, and so much of what they contain may be said to have had Hans's imprimatur.

After his death, Nussy presented me with a vast mass of files and notebooks, diaries and folders, from which I understood just how important this project was to him and how much work he had already done on it down the years. In recreating his autobiography from this material I have tried to do justice to what he might have wanted, but I fear from the copious notes he gave me on the first two chapters that he would have wanted much changed. There may well be errors of fact. Frequently I found more than one account of the same event, and had to decide which was the more probable. Constantly I was trying both to shorten and to simplify, while ensuring that the finished manuscript would read like Professor Kalmus and not like David Benedictus. (Wherever possible I used his own words.) It is not for me to say whether or not I have succeeded. I hope at least that it is not a book of which Hans would have been ashamed.

To Nussy and to Peter (his son), who showed me nothing but kindness and consideration, I owe a debt of gratitude, though my feelings are warmer than that cold phrase implies. But chiefly my gratitude is to Hans Kalmus himself. For it is his personality that I have had to take on, and it is one which came easily and pleasantly to me, like slipping on an old overcoat and feeling comfortable as a result.

David Benedictus
Spring 1990

Preface

One may write the story of one's life from vanity, from a longing for immortality, from a need to justify or excuse one's actions (most common in the case of politicians), or from a variety of other, usually unacknowledged, motives. Many people disapprove of such indulgence. Certainly detachment is not possible in an autobiography. Omissions, inventions and distortions cannot be avoided. Better, many would argue, to leave the writing of one's life-story to others.

However, nobody can have a more complete knowledge of the life and times of an intelligent, mature person than that person himself. And if the old motto on the Temple of Apollo at Delphi is to be credited, the most important thing in life is *gnothi seauton*, to 'know thyself'. So on balance I have concluded that, if a life deserves to be recorded, it should in the first instance, be recorded by the one who has lived it.

As a scientist, I wish to explain to other scientists how I came to research in my chosen areas. For my family, I wish to explain how it felt to be the first of the Kalmus clan to enter the Anglo-Saxon world. I hope too that this book may be of some interest to my pupils and to future scientists and historians.

I have discovered that my major difficulty is what Bertrand Russell described as the 'Tristram Shandy Paradox'. In Sterne's famous novel, Shandy found that it took him two years to write an account of the first two days of his life. He therefore concluded that he would never be able to finish the work since the material would accumulate faster than he could deal with it. Confronted with writing the first 82 years of my life, this is a real problem. The main problem was what to leave out.

Despite the difficulties I have taken the decision to proceed, although this should not imply any exaggerated ideas about my own importance. These pages should be read as just one example of how the extraordinary events of this century have impinged on an individual, a biologist who was forcibly transplanted to the British scientific establishment.

In a corner of an old church in my home town, Prague, the astronomer Tycho Brahe is buried. The grave is rarely visited and the Latin inscription on the tombstone difficult to read in the gloom. I tried it first at the age of twelve, when the Great War was nearing its end. It read: *Nec arma, nec opes – spectra sola pereant*, which translates: 'Not arms, not treasures – only the ghosts of things (ideas) endure.' At the time I did not know the medieval connotations of 'spectrum', and was puzzled; later I was too busy for metaphysical speculations. Now retrospectively I understand that the opposition between the enduring and the changing, which one can read in those mystic words, seem as apposite to an exposition of my life's experience as to that of the eccentric Dane. But there are other Aristotelian opposites . . .

I have tried to balance the space devoted to my life and to my work, to relive the former and to reappraise the latter. I realise that some of my more general conclusions differ from prevailing orthodoxies, and hope that this will not offend but rather add to the interest of the book. Readers not particularly interested in my person or my opinions may nevertheless enjoy some of my descriptions of work and adventure in the laboratory and the wild.

To make my labours intelligible to non-specialist readers I have sometimes had to vulgarise the language of my published work, and to avoid unnecessary embarrassment the identities of a few personalities, whom my book might hurt or damage, have been concealed behind pseudonyms.

Hans Kalmus
Harpenden
1988

1

Austrian Prague

About 30 years ago I received through the post and out of the blue some documents from the Institute for Experimental Pathology in Prague. The Institute bore the same address, 27 Stevens Road, as the house in which I was born a half-century earlier. The papers were relevant to the experiments I was doing at the time. It was a small event, but it illuminated continuities in my life and work, of which I had not been aware. The house had changed its function, so too had I. This strange experience also made me conscious of the strong and often disturbing forces interfering with my development. I thought it might be interesting to review my life as a repeat or control experiment for an earlier one performed on another son of Austrian Prague, Franz Kafka, who named the hero, or anti-hero, of *The Trial*, K, an abbreviation applied to myself by several of my colleagues. Although I deny that we humans are guinea-pigs of some demiurge, it is still worth considering the differences between the two Ks, and trying to understand how differences in time, family tradition and other factors operating in an identical ambience have combined to produce two dissimilar minds. Kafka lived a quiet life in comparatively tranquil times and could afford to be obsessed by prophetic and paranoid ideas, while I had to remain cool and rational if I were to survive several Kafkaesque upheavals. I am not sure whether my attitude is less 'prophetic' than Kafka's, nor whether the incidents told in this book have any relevance for the reader. However, whether serious or funny, they are all true.

I was born in 1906 in what was then Austrian Prague, a provincial baroque town. My parents Ernst and Elsa Kalmus belonged to the then dominant minority, who spoke German, living among half-a-million Czechs. At that time, as indeed for many years after Prague had become the capital of Czechoslovakia, the two groups, though living in close proximity, often in the same tenements, sent their children to separate schools and universities, belonged to different organisations, and patronised different theatres. This curious truce dated back to the Monarchy. *Don Giovanni* had been first performed in our 'old' theatre, where Weber was the conductor. And in the 'new' German theatre Alexander von Zemlinski conducted a full repertoire of operas and symphonies, notably Mozart and Wagner, Mahler and Strauss, but also Schoenberg and Berg. I was never to venture inside the Czech National Theatre, which I passed almost daily and only rarely did I visit a Czech concert. There was no sense of deprivation amongst Germans in Prague. We were 40,000 amongst 500,000, yet we enjoyed a culture rivalling Vienna, Munich or Berlin. Our University was the oldest in the Holy Roman Empire, our technical college was the oldest in the country.

But despite the divisive forces that kept the Czechs and the Germans apart there remained a common sentiment, for which there is no adequate English word, but which in German is called *Heimatgefühl*. This means an attachment to the minutiae of one's early habitat, the streets, the parks, the river, the seasonal festivities, above all the cooking! Through these shared experiences was born a strong communal feeling between 'Pražaks' and 'Pragers', a feeling which has even survived the horrors of the last fifty years, at least among the exiles of my generation.

After my mother's milk dried up, I was fed first by a wet nurse and then artificially. This decision was taken for me by a famous paediatrician in Prague, who – if you believed the rumours – was also treating the members of the Imperial House of Hapsburg. A colleague of my father's, he had been experimenting with buttermilk, which later was to prove ideal for babies. But the effects of it on me were disastrous and I was ill for two years. Among other symptoms I suffered from boils, which were treated with mercury chloride. Consequently I have suffered mercury allergy ever since.

My earliest memory is of the sun shining on the canopy of my pram and the sight of my mother. She was blonde and not only beautiful but so very striking that thirty years later my sister, Mizzi,

2

who was very like her, was approached on the street by a stranger who said 'You must be the daughter of Elsa Kalmus.'

Kalmus is a strange name. I have uncovered half-a-dozen derivations, most of which are undoubtedly wrong. There is a town in Greece with the name of Kalmas, and my Greek friends try to flatter me at times, insisting that I must have originated in Greece. Then the Jewish Department in University College, my academic home in England, maintains that about AD 1000 several rabbinical sages in Rome and Lucca bore the name Kalonymus. They claim me too. More plausible is a derivation from a bitter medicinal root which was sugar-coated and sold in pharmacies. No longer. Alternatively the name could be derived from *Calamus*, the Latin for reed, as used for writing, in which case it is possible that some of my ancestors were scribes. A sector of the human brain is identified as *Calamus Scriptorius*. The possibilities are legion.

The immediate ancestors on my father's side were coffee merchants, and I still remember as a small boy the pleasant smell of coffee roasting in the vaults of the ancestral shop. On the shelves stood huge sugar loaves like soldiers on parade. They were wrapped in brown and blue paper, the white tips naked. There were two competing stores belonging to the Kalmus family, on the opposite corners of the Lange Gasse in the Old City. On one it said 'S. Kalmus', which spoken aloud made 'Ess Kalmus' ('Eat Kalmus'). On the other: 'S. K. Kalmus', which sounded like 'Ess ka Kalmus' ('Don't Eat Kalmus'). This rather fatuous joke became very well known, and probably provided useful publicity for both stores.

My maternal grandfather, Max John, lived in Budapest; he plied tug-boats on the Danube, one of which was named Elsa after my mother. I have seen it in use. His wife, Berta Fuchs, was Viennese. She was the only grandparent I knew.

In the years preceding the First World War, the seasons were still orderly. There were no strawberries in January and there was no skating in August. A safe circle carried one through the year from the summer holidays, through the fruit harvest in the autumn to the Christmas tree, and on into the warmth of spring. I could be confident that in June there would be cherries, bright red ones for eating raw, and dark mysterious ones for finding in cakes. My father would take me swimming in the river and on one special evening every year there would be fireworks in honour of the 'Saint on the Bridge', St John of Nepomuk.

The first year I was permitted to attend the fireworks was 1909. I was just three years old. My father was too busy to accompany me, and since my mother was not fond of crowds, it fell to Mrs Mushikova, the cook, and Jirina, the maid, to take me out. On the familiar quay near the weir and the medieval bridge, in view of the castle and the cathedral across the river, promenaded hundreds of people, soldiers and old men, boys and girls, grandmothers and children. When the press became such that I could no longer see, the good-natured Jirina put me on her shoulders.

I remember a hiss above the water and something which let off orange sparks rising into the leaden sky, slowing down, and then, faintly glowing, falling gently into the depths. Before I could ask about this miracle a second such thing rose into the sky, but this was even more startling, for, at the highest point of its trajectory, amid loud detonations, it released clusters of red, blue and green stars, before vanishing as silently as the first. What could it be? '*Rako-mejtle*' (fireworks), explained Jirina. We spoke German at home of course, and I knew little Czech. I was content that what I had seen was a *rakomejtle*.

In the January of the following year I ceased to be fed in the nursery. Seated at mealtimes at my parents' table I could listen to their talk: domestic affairs, political news, novelties. One such novelty was a thing called a comet, which one could see moving through the nights and which had a shiny tail. Obviously, I thought, this is a *rakomejtle*. Rockets and comets (*Raketen und Kometen*) were the same and this one too I had to see.

There was much curiosity in Prague about the appearance of Halley's Comet, not only curiosity but apprehension too. Obscurantists and charlatans delighted in predicting the end of the world. On the evening of the day when it was reputably reported that the comet would at last be visible, I crept out of bed onto the balcony and searched the sky for a *rakomejtle*. There was nothing. At breakfast the next morning my mother suggested that we might perhaps go to Charles Square that evening and search the sky with her opera glasses (of which she was particularly proud), but my father came up with an even better idea. Among his patients was an assistant at the old Jesuit Observatory.

At the place where Tycho Brahe and Kepler had made their observations, I was placed on a chair and made to look through a telescope aimed at the comet. It was my first great disappointment, and more vitally it was a disappointment with science. All I saw amongst the wealth of stars in the sky was a not particularly bright star with a pale tail. It was quite unremarkable. It did not move and neither did it sparkle, hiss or explode.

In my later life *Raketen und Kometen* were to develop a startling new relationship. In about 1930 I saw on a colleague's desk models of moon rockets. Later in London I was to experience German rockets and to watch on my television the first Russian satellites, the first Americans stepping onto the moon.

But something has fundamentally changed. My long remembered rockets were flung into the air and returned to earth. Not any more. Hundreds of satellites are now in orbit and following the rules, formulated by Kepler and Newton, which govern the movements not only of the planets but also of comets and rockets.

Friends and family participated in the development of this branch of science. A colleague invented propellants for space ships; one of my sons lectures on astrophysics; my grandchildren have studied moon dust under the microscope. Days and seasons are no longer universal. For the crews of the spaceships days last minutes; the words winter and summer will have no meaning. It seems a long way from Prague in 1909.

When at the age of 17 I first became interested in genetics I was exposed to a grotesque incident which has made me wary ever since of accepting other scientists' results without checking them for myself. One day (and I am talking now of a time just after the First World War) a young colleague of my father's, who was investigating paternity tests, visited our house, and wanted to test us for blood groups, a newish discipline in those days. He duly took some blood from my parents, my brother, my sister and myself, and went away. He returned the following day with a rather sheepish manner, which was explained when we learned that according to his findings neither my sister nor I could be our father's offspring. We were all somewhat embarrassed and further tests were undertaken, when it became clear that neither of us could be my mother's children either!

I was to recall this incident thirty years later when after the Second

5

World War we learned that almost 10 per cent of the blood group determinations of the American army had been incorrect.

To return to my family and my early years. After the premature death of my grandfather, my father had had a struggle to get through medical school. He was 37 years old when I was born and 69 when I saw him last. He was a small, slender man, rather bald but with the neat, pointed beard that was customary at the time. This, with his fine features and blue-grey eyes, made him appear quite distinguished. He was a mild man, compassionate but austere, greatly overworked throughout his working life. Only rarely did he raise his voice and he never hit my brother, my sister or myself, although his authority was very clear to all of us. I remember at the age of 15 bringing him my school report which, unusually, included two slightly critical remarks. He just pointed at them with his finger and asked: 'What is that?' It was never necessary for him to do so again.

He was a late child, the only surviving son but with three sisters considerably older than himself. He often claimed that he had had four mothers. When he was 12 his father died, at a time when the family firm and fortunes had barely recovered from the slump after the Franco-Prussian War; his elderly and ailing mother was left comparatively poor. As a consequence there was considerable family resistance when he declared that he intended to follow a brother-in-law and study medicine. It could not have been easy for him, having to earn money by coaching while studying and counting every penny. In the event he just missed the ultimate accolade *summa cum laude sub auspiciis imperatoris* when he failed to get a distinction in just one discipline, forensic medicine. Ironically this was to be his vocation. After some junior appointments in surgery and neurology/psychiatry and a stint as assistant to Hofrat Pick, he became a police surgeon and a medical expert in the lawcourts. Later he became interested in what was then the unfashionable subject, 'mental health', and in industrial hygiene, which he taught at the German Technical University. As a result of my father's occupation I was brought into contact with a great variety of people – criminals, the mentally disturbed, the police – whom middle-class children rarely meet.

I recall my father smoking a cigar, as he sat at his desk, absorbed in papers and nearly oblivious of my presence. On several occasions I would be told to wait for him at an entrance to the police headquarters. Being forgetful, he would leave by another door and set off on other errands. It would be some hours before the police took me home.

I do not know what my father can have been thinking of when he took me at the age of five to a rural station near the Carinthian capital, Klagenfurt, where there was a small population of women suffering from extreme goitres. Not only were they severely deformed, but their behaviour was highly eccentric, for their conversation was inarticulate and their actions sinister and abnormal. It came close to a childish vision of Dante's *Inferno*, and it made a lasting impression on me, far stronger in fact than the professional encounters I was to have in later life with psychotic and mentally defective people. I was certainly frightened by what I saw, but I think that I was more disturbed and interested than frightened.

Although I sometimes heard about the courts and the criminally insane, my father seldom discussed his work with me, and never, where his post-mortems were concerned. He performed thousands of these. I was no more than eight when I first used his microscope. The problem he was then investigating was whether it was possible to determine from the condition of the lungs whether a body dragged from the river had been drowned, or killed and then dumped in the water. Only in the first case would there be any diatoms in the lungs. So my early exercise in microscopy was searching for diatoms in macerated lung tissue. My father also studied what could be learned from bloodstains, and introduced a method of crystallising blood into what were called haemochromogens, which I could admire under the polarising microscope. Much later I read a paper of my father's in quite a different branch of forensic science, a monograph on pathological lying. When I doubted some of the reported cases he told me that such incredible flights of fantasy were only extreme forms of deviation from the truth, common to all people, even scientists.

Despite his long hours he found time to pursue other concerns. He liked swimming. On rare Sunday afternoons in summer we would take a family trip on one of the steamboats which puffed their way up and down the Moldau (Vltava) River. He was a diabetic in the difficult days before insulin, and, though small, had been an excellent horseman and fencer. At that time in a German university it was useful to have a reputation as a good fencer.

7

My beautiful mother was a more extrovert person. She was the disciplinarian in the family, even occasionally boxing our ears. On the other hand it was easier to discuss problems with her than with my father.

I knew very little of my mother's childhood and adolescence. She had grown up in Budapest in the heyday of that city's prosperity and frivolity, first with a beloved Hungarian father, and, after his early death, in the care of a Viennese mother, who had limited intelligence and whose circumstances were needy. My mother must have come to hate this ambience, for, though she obtained a teacher's certificate and even taught for a year in a Budapest school, she never spoke Hungarian to us, but only German, her mother's tongue. Indeed, my grandmother herself had never managed to speak Hungarian during more than 30 years in Budapest. Such paradoxical situations were quite common in the diverse national centres of the Austro-Hungarian monarchy; in Prague also.

My mother never really mastered Czech. A most important episode in her early life concerned a month which she spent in Rome with her class-mates during her last year at college. There she acquired a lifelong interest in antiquity, Renaissance and Baroque, an interest she later developed and enlarged in Prague. She bought with her pocket-money a picture of the bust of the young Augustus, the first thing which I saw every morning. Many years later I was to learn that she must have married my father on the rebound from some unhappy romance. I think that they were none too compatible, but they stayed together until their tragic, violent death during the Second World War. Her emotional conflicts were, as in most orderly families, entirely concealed from us children. I found amongst her papers poems and short stories of great poignancy, though, I am sorry to say, of little aesthetic merit. She must have had periods of great unhappiness.

After her marriage she involved herself increasingly in charitable and political organisations. During the First World War she organised a charity for the Galician refugees from the Eastern provinces which had been overrun by the Russians. On one occasion they refused to give their children the milk provided for them by the charity, because it was not kosher, and poured it away, to the great annoyance of the Czech neighbours. The President of the charity, a Countess Goudenov, had the generous notion of presenting to the unfortunate refugees two of her beautiful angora goats. It fell to me to take these goats to the outskirts of Prague and I did so, accompanied by a policeman. I still remember masses of jeering people making fun of us, as we, a small boy and a policeman, led these spectacular animals down Wenceslas Square.

My mother, whose political acumen was greater than most people's, certainly greater than mine, was an avid reader, and belonged to a club of some 20 women, who bought the latest novels and circulated them amongst themselves. Thus I had the opportunity of reading a good deal of contemporary literature, both in German and translated from French, English and other languages. Most unusually for that time she enrolled as a mature student to study philosophy at the University. She was also a season ticket holder at the German theatre, and subscribed to the chamber music concerts on Sunday mornings. In later years she loved the movies, especially the comics, and delighted in Harold Lloyd and Charlie Chaplin. And it was her connections with the Women's International League for Peace and Freedom that were to prove invaluable in gaining me entry into England when things became desperate.

The situation of a child in a multilingual environment is both rich and complicated. I remember, when I was about three or four, I had a vivacious children's maid whom I greatly loved. She was very friendly with some policemen and did not always want to have me around when they visited or met her in the park. So she devised some little means of keeping me away and one of the policemen used to send me to a grocer's shop with a one kreutzer coin to buy myself a chocolate cigar. However she did not say 'chocolate cigar' in Czech, but said I should buy some 'brains' (*rozumi*). The first time I undertook this transaction it was in her presence and I received a nice little chocolate cigar with a red ribbon at the end. So I subsequently did when I went alone. One day however someone whom I had not seen before was serving in the shop, and had no idea what to serve me. When I pointed at the cigars which were displayed on the counter general hilarity ensued. Upset, I complained to my parents who could not help but laugh, though they did reprimand the maid.

Having two or more languages has a profound effect. It has often been said with justification that one cannot properly master one's mother tongue if one has not learnt Latin. Being bi- or multilingual leads to a kind of compartmentalisation. I learned to swear and to speak to children in Czech. I know the systematics of fish in French, because I was taught this at Roscoff Marine Station in Brittany. I am none too certain in my German terminology when dealing with genetics, and I do not know the names of many of the simple tools in English, nor the vernacular names of many plants in the wild.

When I was four-and-a-half my mother became pregnant again and I was taken away by my grandmother to stay in a spa. Upon my return I found my little sister, Marie ('Mizzi'), and a joyous atmosphere in the house. I clearly remember watching my mother nursing her and asking me whether I wanted a little milk too, an offer which I declined with the greatest scorn. Three years later, just before the outbreak of the war, my brother, Ernst, was born. Not ideal timing, and indeed he was to suffer somewhat from malnutrition. There was rationing and a black market, based on barter. I recall a revolting type of bread, baked mainly from maize. Potatoes were our staple diet, although sometimes there were treats, as, for instance, when my uncle, who was in the Hungarian army, arrived with a barrel of plum jam for us, and, even more vital, a huge tin of lard, which we would spread on the potatoes to make them more palatable. When Ernst saw his first orange he didn't even realise that it was something which could be eaten. My mother, who was always slim, ate little.

Though a weakly child and in some ways timid, I did not lack self-confidence. I remember once being asked what I wanted to be when I grew up and saying that I wanted to be Emperor. It was pointed out to me at once, of course, that I wasn't a Hapsburg, and that the monarchy was hereditary, to which I replied: 'Well, what is next best after Emperor?' They told me prime minister, so I said all right, I would be prime minister. Strange, because since then I have never had any political ambitions or inclinations at all.

To my siblings I was a typical older brother, and truthfully did not much care for them; until they were both well into their adolescent years we kept out of one another's way. Later we were to take skiing holidays together and now, far from home, we have become close friends.

Every summer the family would take itself off to the Alps for a month or more, and it was during these holidays that my love of mountains was nurtured. For much of the time I would wander off on my own, roaming the woods, the lakeshores, and the hills, collecting butterflies, observing the animals, and the behaviour of ants.

It was while we were on our summer holiday in 1914 that war was declared. It was harvest time and I remember Count Kinsky, a local landowner, posting the Emperor Franz Josef's declaration of war against Serbia on the garden gates. It was addressed to all his people – in 19 languages. A copy of this remarkable document is displayed in London's Imperial War Museum.

Although I was told at the age of nine about my Jewish origins, I was not really aware of any Jewishness, and the only orthodox Jews I ever came across were strange Polish refugees. There had been occasional outbreaks of anti-semitism in Bohemia, notably the Hübner case, involving the familiar accusation of ritual murder, but these were forgotten.

I was brought up in the Protestant faith, and attended an excellent Lutheran school, which was in no way sectarian; there were a few Catholics and Jews in my class. Nevertheless, Luther's figure loomed large and his famous saying at the Diet of Worms: 'Here I stand. I cannot do otherwise. God help me' has remained throughout my life a paradigm for my behaviour.

The kind of school it was may perhaps be best illustrated by describing one particular occasion. In the second form I was selected to declaim the story of Christ's birth at the school's Christmas celebration. When I started to memorise St Matthew's text, I asked the teacher why Augustus should have wanted to 'count' – not 'tax' as in the English Bible – all the people; and so at a very early age I was taught something about census-taking and statistics. At the end of my performance the shepherds' adoration was rendered by a *Gloria* from the school choir. It must have been a modest enough effort but its impact has lasted to this day. The radiant atmosphere protected me from any kind of stage fright, and I have never since suffered from this disability.

It is important to realise that Prague at that time was predominantly Catholic. It was known as 'the golden town of the hundred towers'. There were Romanesque and Gothic churches and monasteries, but it was the baroque of the Reformation and Counter-Reformation which gave, and gives, the old town its character.

11

In the schools a very different history was taught, depending upon whether the establishment was Czech or German. The question was hotly debated as to whether or not Bohemia had been vacated by the Germanic Marcomanni before the Czechs arrived. It may seem an academic debate, but the implications were rather more serious.

We Germans learned little about the Przemyslids or the Hussites, while Czech children hardly knew that Prague had once been the capital of medieval Germany or that as late as 1848 Bohemia sent delegates to the revolutionary parliament in Frankfurt. Who had been the builders of the Gothic and Baroque buildings, which they passed daily, was not clear to them. Thus they would be quite unprepared when old powerful forces, in the terrible form of Hitler's army, overwhelmed them.

Falsification of history by propagandists is ubiquitous, and so is its rewriting. For those on the sidelines the results are sometimes grotesque. When visiting Kos, I discovered that the two most conspicuous buildings of this Greek island's capital – mosques – were not to be found on the official map of the town. In the pictorial history in the Rivera Museum in Mexico the maize-worshipping Indians are immediately followed by the revolutionaries of 1910–20. Four centuries of Spanish rule and culture are omitted.

The first lesson I received that there can be a more sober and objective approach to history came when I first visited England. One of the London sights that made the greatest impact on me was Parliament Square. There in front of the government building was the statue of Richard the Lionheart; there too the statue of Cromwell. In Prague we would not have been mature enough to realise that history cannot be partial. But to return to my schooldays . . .

My teachers at the grammar school do not appear in retrospect particularly eminent, but those who taught me Classics did instil in me a feeling for classical antiquity, which was of great benefit when I came to travel in Greece and Italy.

I had considerable problems with my Latin, the first language I had to learn from scratch, and the problems were not much helped by the first teacher to introduce me to this subject, a barely Germanised Czech. He was amiable but shallow and my mother was far more helpful. She devised a box in which a number of little cards could be placed. On one side of each card I wrote a Latin word and on the other the German translation, and, at the end of each homework session I would take out some twenty or so of these cards and, having found the Latin or German equivalent, put them in another box. By this ingenious means I gradually acquired a working Latin vocabulary.

But grammar was not so easily acquired. My father did his best, but he had forgotten most of what Latin he had once had, and an expert was called in. Looking like Michelangelo's Moses, he was an impressive figure, but turned out to be a professor of paediatrics, not of Classical languages. I was just 10, but already I had seen an emperor without his clothes. There were to be many more such emperors.

Our Greek teacher, Professor Sturm was a more considerable – and more controversial – figure. We called him *'koza'*, the Czech for goat on account of his high-pitched voice and red beard. Although he was a real enthusiast for everything Hellenic, and could describe his adventures in Greece with a brilliance of observation, I found his teaching methods insupportable, and we had a running feud. But I was to get my revenge. In due course, by the time I got to university, I had also become a ski instructor, and as luck would have it I was the instructor chosen to teach Professor Sturm and his class when they came on holiday to the Riesengebirge. Thus it fell to me to stand at the bottom of the slope and whistle, and for Professor Sturm to descend at my bidding, and frequently perform a nosedive in front of me. But he took it in excellent humour and we became good friends.

I have in my possession a school photograph from those days of 28 of my class-mates. Many of them perished in the Second World War or in the Holocaust; the survivors were dispersed over every continent. They have fought in at least six armies, sometimes on opposing sides. Some have been persecutors, others victims of persecution, one or two both. Few have managed a consistent career; fewer have brought up children. Only one is still alive.

Among the Jews who suffered the terrible but unrecorded fate of millions of others were two beautiful and bright girls with whom most of the boys had been in love at one time or another. Of the survivors one of my closest friends lost his wife and two sons in the gas-chambers, and was himself liberated by the Russians. He had become a member of the Czech Communist Party and for a short while had had in his charge a large part of the Czech textile industry before he was removed. Another, who attained even greater eminence, was lucky to escape prosecution and probable death in the infamous trials of the fifties.

Of those who escaped, one, a writer and poet, found England intolerable and returned home, where he became a guide at Prague's Jewish museum. He emigrated a second time, and lives with his Czech wife and student son in a small town in Upper Bavaria, where he writes nostalgically of times long past.

Then there was the man who returned from Russia and became artistic director of the Czech National Theatre, where productions of Shakespeare still employ his translations into modern Czech. His translations of German poetry are less well known. He drowned many years ago in the Black Sea. One of his two brothers became the principal orthopaedic surgeon to the Israeli army, the other was an officer in the French Foreign Legion.

Another character, a gifted dentist, was offered a post in Edinburgh shortly before the occupation of Prague. He returned home and perished. A research chemist, with whom I had often skied in the Bohemian mountains, was to become a diplomat. Appointed Czech cultural attaché in London he was considered *persona non grata*, and was expelled for spying. He died in Prague in poverty and distress.

Two luckier men were lawyers. One came to England where he built up an international law agency, the other a flourishing glove factory. Of two doctors one became a neuro-surgeon in California, the other a urologist in upstate New York.

The only 'religious' Jew in our class became a rabbi in north London. I met him on Hampstead Heath shortly after the fall of France. At first he hurried towards me, then suddenly turned and walked away. He obviously disapproved of me.

Most of my non-Jewish class-mates stayed in Prague during the Nazi occupation and some of them prospered. But their tragedy was only delayed. After the Russians had driven out the Nazis, the Czechs summarily deprived all German-speakers like myself of their rights and expelled them. Thus were created three-and-a-half million refugees, of whom only a few were 'readmitted'. Amongst these was the son of an old Prague family, who had kept faith with his Jewish wife and managed to save her life. Another, a tennis player and skier, was even appointed sports editor of the Communist national paper, *Rude Pravo*. Another found employment in the Statistical Office. He died recently while on holiday in America.

Among those who had to leave Prague, several had been doctors in the German army. Two survived the Russian winter as soldiers. So far as I can ascertain none of my class-mates was powerful in any Nazi organisation, but there were several other of my friends who were. My fellow lecturer in the Zoology Department, with whom I had collaborated on research and climbed in the Alps, was already an SS officer on the day he 'helped' me leave my room after I had been expelled from the university. He died miserably in the third year of the war.

Then there was the younger colleague with whom I had played violin duets. He became a real Nazi, and later weeded out all non-Aryans. The war over, he took Holy Orders and died as a missionary doctor amongst the South African blacks. His advice to me had been to divorce my wife, abandon my children, and apply to the Führer for 'aryanisation'. I presume he meant well.

2

Czechoslovakia Between the Wars

One evening late in August 1918 when out rabbiting with the parson of a village in North Bohemia, I heard bursts of gunfire from the Western Front, some 500 kilometres away. The guns were quite loud, like thunder. It was my first experience of the realities of war.

On the morning of 28 October 1918, my father telephoned my mother from police headquarters, where he was on duty as medical officer. He told her that on no account should she or we leave the house; there were crowds tearing down the Austrian double-headed eagles from official buildings. There had been singing and shouting to mark the end of many centuries of Hapsburg rule in Bohemia, but the transition was remarkably peaceful, and I don't believe there was a single casualty. The Tyrolean and Hungarian regiments left the city, after which there was a lull, during which we watched and wondered: what would happen to us?

What happened was a visit a few days later from Dr Prokop, the head of a revolutionary committee which had been investigating the servants of the old regime. Fortunately my father was not only fluent in Czech, but was renowned for his humane attitude to his work and had a reputation for being entirely non-political. Consequently he was permitted to stay on.

The other changes, as and when they came, were not so alarming. Outside our house my father was required to remove the name-plate which gave his title and degree in German. The German names had already disappeared from the streets during the first few days of the bloodless revolution, as had the advertisements for German theatres and cultural events. More upsetting was the closure of

German schools and the confiscation of our own school building. My beautiful grammar school, close by St Stephens Cathedral, became the office of the Tobacco Monopoly. Thereafter my education took place mostly during the afternoons in the class-rooms of other schools, which were often a distance apart, and always over-crowded.

The dismemberment of the Hapsburg monarchy, hailed in the West as a great liberation for the smaller nations of Europe, may with hindsight be seen as one of the major disasters of European history, opening the doors to Hitler and Communism. Being a victim, I certainly had a sharper eye for the deficiencies and hypocrisies of the new regime than my Czech contemporaries who gloried in the new situation. It took them 20 years to be disillusioned.

A few weeks after the end of the war came the triumphal entry into Prague of the first President of the Republic, T. G. Masaryk. My father, on duty as usual, pulled strings to get me a place on a police lorry which was supervising the parade, so I was witness to the enthusiasm with which he was greeted. Twenty years later I witnessed his farewells only a short time before the fall of his Republic. In an interview he gave in the thirties Masaryk was to explain why he had not taken the Nazi threat more seriously. All his life, he said, he had had the din of Pan-German agitation in his ears, and he refused to overrate its significance now. When a journalist pointed out that not until Hitler had the Pan-Germans been in a position of power, he remarked: 'You journalists, you smoke too much, you drink too much, and so you constantly exaggerate danger.' He was to pay dearly for his mistake.

Although my parents had lost all their savings, which as patriots they had invested in War Loans, we were spared the worst ravages of the inflation that was to infect Germany and Austria. We were also able to live securely, though modestly, on my father's salary as a police surgeon and on whatever he could earn as an expert in psychiatry and forensic medicine. My mother was fully committed to her charitable work and her literary society.

After 1918 it was always made quite clear to me that I belonged to a second-class minority. The days when German students like my father had had to hide in attics had long since gone, but on several occasions I was spat at and reminded that as a 'Jew'

17

(synonymous at the time with 'German' so far as the Czech mob was concerned) I would be left only with 'the shit'. What a terrible prophecy for both Germans and Jews in Prague.

Other members of our family found themselves under siege. The industrial complex of which my uncle was a leading manager found itself subject to five different legislatures, with its component parts often divided by complicated tariff barriers.

It is an interesting question who suffered most from the petty discriminations which existed in Czechoslovakia after 1918. Naturally, the Republic favoured Czech institutions, but many German ones managed to keep up standards. Czech patients thronged the clinics of the German universities, graduates of our Technical College were everywhere in demand, and the cultural life of the German-speaking community continued to flourish.

Czech scientists, scholars and artists, though better off materially, increasingly cut themselves off from other local researchers, and turned instead to the universities of England and America. Textbooks had to be written in Czech, although these were often little more than compilations from existing works in other languages, and new technical terms had to be invented.

As for myself, I had more than enough school work, along with remedial orthopaedic sessions and piano instruction, and found myself in a kind of apathy, having little contact with the Czech-speaking citizens around me. Not that I minded. Like most of my friends, I was convinced that my German culture was superior.

My piano teacher had the imposing name of Johann Edward Hubner. He looked like J. S. Bach and wrote oratorios, but he was not a great fan of his lowliest pupil. My problem with him (and with his successor) was that I had no interest in practice. I could sight-read pretty well, and would happily plough my way through the Beethoven Sonatas, but exercises were merely tiresome.

In school I had a variety of teachers, amongst whom I found the Classicists the most sympathetic. I was one of the very few children who took the Classics seriously, but none the less I did have a considerable contretemps with my Greek teacher about Oedipus. My teacher seemed unable to appreciate the difference between a Greek tragedy and a family drama.

I also took exception to calculus, and announced, reasonably politely, that I thought it was a swindle. The maths master, an old

18

pedant, should perhaps have recognised that this was a more intelligent response than those pupils who merely tried to get the sums to come out right. I did not then know – and nor, of course, did he – that greater minds than my own had had the greatest of difficulty with differential calculus. A letter from Bertrand Russell to Gilbert Murray, written in December 1902, argued that any book on calculus would a priori contain lies. I feel that if the author of *Principia Mathematica* had difficulties with the logic of calculus, then a 16-year-old had every right to have comparable qualms.

Gymnastics flourished at the grammar school, but nothing that today we would call organised sport. I was interested enough, however, to join a hockey club, and I played full back. But I hated tying myself down to definite times and particular dates, as a consequence of which I only played in the reserves.

Athletics I took far more seriously, and it turned out that I had a real talent for track events. When I lined up to run, people would smile because of my unimpressive posture, but after I had won the 100 metres by three or four metres, it was a different story. I was a natural sprinter with Olympic qualifying times, acknowledged to be the fastest man in Prague, perhaps in the Republic, with my picture in the popular magazines. But athletics meetings in Prague were not always happy affairs and I was often booed by Czech supporters. Once when I ran the final leg in the 4 × 100 metres relay, spectators invaded the track and an attempt was made to trip me. In any case I was more interested in my work, and, in due course, my future wife. So when the 1924 Olympics came along, I told the club that I had no interest in participating.

At the beginning of this century scientific research was not an established profession, biology did not exist as a unified subject, and naturalists were amateurs. My father had done some early work on the haemochromogenes, microscopic crystals derived from the red blood pigment of animals and characteristic of the species, and had published papers on his psychiatric/forensic matters, but these were by-products of his professional work. My mother's background was industrial and commercial, her interests literary and political. I had no clear idea what research work involved and no inkling until well into my teens that I might become a scientist. But a pattern was emerging.

19

An elderly aunt whom I sometimes visited had a collection of popular scientific books, left behind by children who had grown up. Among them was a large volume describing various geological periods, which were illustrated with colour plates. These fanciful reconstructions of marine biotics, populated by trilobites or huge saurians, of tropical swamps with fern and horsetail, of glaciated landscapes dotted with mammoths, reindeer and cave bears had fired my imagination in my pre-school days, long before I became interested in living animals and plants. There was no zoo in Prague at that time, and with the exception of the 'Sternbergeum', a collection in the geological department named after a friend of Goethe, the museums had little to offer. A city child, I only saw nature during the summer holidays.

But during the First World War I spent two summers with the junior pastor of our congregation and his family in their small villa on the shore of Lake Hirschberg in Northern Bohemia. Like so many of his English counterparts, Pastor Wolf had interested himself in the local flora and fauna and kept many books on the subject in his house. But there were practical reasons too to get out into the fields. Food rations needed to be supplemented and substitutes for coffee and tea had to be found. So off I went into the woods to collect berries and mushrooms and herbs for tea and acorns for coffee. During those forays I inevitably acquired a working knowledge also of the wildlife, the butterflies and beetles, although I never became a serious collector – of anything.

Also I read. My father had given me a subscription to the monthly magazine, *Kosmos*, at that time the leading journal of popular science. Four or five times a year *Kosmos* would publish more specialised monographs which were often of considerable merit.

Perhaps because I received so little help in biology at school, I had preferred the exact sciences to naturalist pursuits; it was a time when everybody was focusing their attention on relativity, atomic physics and biochemistry. But at about that time Dr Friedl Pick, a friend of my parents and a keen amateur palaeontologist rekindled my interest in extinct life forms by taking me to the nearby fossil sites in the Bohemian palaeozoic. Usually we found little, but there was always the thrill of anticipation, the possibility of uncovering with one's hammer an object no human eye had ever seen before, and which had been hidden in an envelope of stone for millions of years, a graptolite in a slab of slate perhaps, or a trilobite in a concretion. Ever since, I have preferred exploration and discovery to plodding research. Once, when cleaving slate in a sun-baked quarry, I saw a most beautiful dark plant imprinted on the freshly exposed light face. But when I lifted the slate the 'fossil' had gone; it had only been the shadow of a woody herb and of no concern to me.

When it was time to consider what subjects I should study at university my interest in fossils surfaced again. I was influenced by Dr Pick presenting me with a book *Palaeobiology* by the Viennese zoologist, Othenio Abel. The book was full of interesting speculations about extinct animals and parts of it read like a detective story. I settled on palaeontology and geology much against the wishes of my father, who tried to persuade me at least to combine geology with mining. When I refused to change my mind, my father accused me of being just too lazy to take an examination in descriptive geometry, a subject which I had not studied at the classical grammar school but which was required by the technical university. So I sat down with my friend and schoolmate, Fritz Hellman, who very definitely did want to study at the 'Tech', and spent a month of the summer reading and drawing. Then we both took and passed the requisite exam. I presented my father with the certificate, but insisted on sticking to my original plan. He gave in.

My absurd preference for fossil life stayed with me until the end of my first university year when I transferred to zoology. The physiologist, Richard Kahn, a friend of my father, helped me to this decision. When I complained about the tedium of scrutinising drawers full of silurian corals and memorising so many names, he explained to me the difference between what he called 'necrological' sciences and biology. I particularly remember him paraphrasing Rutherford by saying that collecting and identifying fossils was like stamp collecting, useful for the stratigraphic geologist, but of no biological interest. Also one could not experiment with fossils. That did the trick. I transferred to zoology – and ended up studying medicine.

Quite untutored was an early interest in ants. Before I started school I would be taken by our maid for a walk, sometimes to a park on the Sophia Island in the Moldau (Vltava) River. This was reached by a bridge from the embankment which was too narrow for vehicles, so that I could roam freely while the maid was gossiping

21

with the other maids. I could observe thrushes, sparrows and pigeons on the lawns, crows in the trees, the gulls over the river. With these creatures I could not make contact, but I could play with those that crawled on the gravel paths and on the stones of the walls which encircled the park; with slugs, with centipedes and with beetles. But mostly I experimented with ants. There was no shortage. Sometimes they marched singly, sometimes in counter currents – larger black ones and smaller reds. On one occasion I remember seeing them carrying pupae, eggs as I thought, in one direction while marching empty-handed in the opposite direction. For hours I would try to divert these columns, putting twigs or stones in their way, and also to remove ants from their pupae. I asked numerous questions about these ants, but nobody could, or would, answer them, and so my interest died.

Forty years later when I observed leaf-cutting ants and army ants in the tropics, I had access to books, and learned a little more about the intricate behaviour of ants and their societies. But I have worked only with a representative of the other group of social hymenoptera, the honey bee.

There was another branch of biology to which I was introduced in a rather roundabout way. Exploring rivers and streams in which people might have drowned, my father became an expert on freshwater diatoms, and I was introduced to the use of plankton nets and mud scrapers. I was as familiar with fresh-water life, as others were familiar with birds. This was to be my particular study and for 10 years I was to be in charge of practical classes in freshwater biology, and the subject of my thesis was to be the seasonal cycles of life at the bottom of Prague's river.

These encounters with scientific matters aroused my wonderment, fed my imagination, and remained lodged permanently in my memory. But there was only one problem which encouraged me to pursue specific questions.

In my tenth year I discovered that the formula H_2O which I had come across in one of my father's textbooks of chemistry stood for water. My father explained that it meant that two atoms of hydrogen and one atom of oxygen combined to produce one molecule of water. He then told me what atoms and molecules were. I asked to see them and when he told me that that was not possible I further inquired how therefore one could know that exactly two hydrogen atoms combined with one of oxygen; why not one with one? Either he did not know the answer or I did not understand his explanation. Then on my tenth birthday I received a book of experiments, in which was an illustrated item about electrolysis. If one applied electricity to a weak solution of table salt (the book said) one obtained 'twice as much' of the gas hydrogen as of the gas oxygen. Clearly this had some reference to my chemistry formula, but what? Reading on I learned that if one joined the two gases one could ignite the mixture with a match, and produce not just water but also a loud bang. Obviously electrolysis was an experiment well worth undertaking.

My parents were out for the evening, and cook was also absent. Undisturbed I went to the kitchen, filled a tumbler from the tap and put a coffee spoon of salt in it. Then I took the tumbler to my father's study, switched off his table-lamp and cut the wires with a pair of scissors. Then I dipped the two ends of the wire into the tumbler of water and switched on. There was a bang and a spark. But what alarmed me even more was the complete darkness, not only in the study, but also in the rest of the flat, with the exception of one room – my own. There was nothing I could do but await my parents' return and confess. As it was my birthday and I had only been following the book they had given me, I got off lightly. My mother warned me against 'such dangerous experiments', and my father explained that what had happened had merely been a short, adding that in any case the alternating current from the mains could not have separated the hydrogen and the oxygen. But he was puzzled as to why there was still light and current in my room. It transpired that my room had originally been a part of the flat now occupied by a neighbour and the electricity for my room had never been disconnected from his meter. The fault was rectified quickly but it was years before I fully understood the laws which explain why chemists write H_2O for water.

There were other interests which I developed in my teens which were to take up considerable amounts of my time. There were skiing and mountaineering, and photography – in which I won several prizes. But as in so many areas professionalism had become all-important and anything the amateur could hope to achieve was meaningless by comparison with the pictures published in colour magazines and periodicals.

Military service was compulsory even in peacetime. With great misgivings I joined the army, but not for long. My allergies came to my rescue, and I reacted violently against the straw sacks on which the recruits were expected to sleep. My asthmatic attacks and sneezing fits were so disruptive that I was sent to a military hospital for investigation. Traces of tuberculosis were found, and, after a brief holiday at a sanatorium, I was dismissed from the army. Just as well. The Czech army was never to fire a shot in anger when Hitler invaded the country, and the Supreme Commander, President Benes, Masaryk's successor, fled to England, as I did. There I would be able to contribute to the fight against Hitler without wearing a uniform.

Growing up in the young Czechoslovak democracy affected me in several ways. Freedom of expression, freedom of travel and equality before the law were, I assumed, normal conditions of life. But they were no longer automatic and there was no ignoring the blacker side, the bureaucratic corruption, the deep hostilities between the various Czech factions, the hypocritical discrimination against German speakers. But it appears to me now that such flaws in the system were far less destructive than the 'honest passions' of the Nazis' own criminal extremists who were waiting in the wings.

La Rochefoucauld has described hypocrisy as the compliment which vice pays to virtue, and it is implicit in hypocrisy that the hypocrite is aware of the moral imperatives which he or she is violating. The existence of hypocrisy also contradicts the notion (emphatically repudiated by Plato) that ignorance is the sole source of evil behaviour, although it certainly contributes. Jesus's dictum: 'Father forgive them, for they know not what they do' does not apply to hypocrites.

What is undeniable is that growing up as a young man in an imperfect democracy taught me how to cope with inconsistencies in whatever society I later found myself in; and with contradictions in my own personality.

It scarcely needs to be added that the chief advantage of living in Czechoslovakia at that time was that I was shielded from the murderous attentions of Nazism in Austria and Germany. Then, as throughout my life, I sought solace in the mountains, and, whenever conditions permitted it, on skis. There were hills around Prague and fine skiing in the Riesengebirge, the mountain range in the north-east of Bohemia, with a top peak of 1,600 metres.

My first attempt to ski was a disaster. I went with a friend who had spent some time in the Tyrol, and bought myself a pair of skis. The first time I tried them out, I broke one immediately. Not daring to tell my parents I left the skis with one of my colleagues living near the station. The broken one was primitively repaired by an old man in the mountains and I used that damaged ski for some two years. My enthusiasm remained undiminished. With a few class-mates and some colleagues from the University I would take off for a few days cross-country skiing under the tutelage, initially, of a Norwegian instructor.

On one occasion two of us were out very late and skiing above the timber line when we saw an enormously bright star and thought that we had made a great astronomical discovery, a 'Nova'. It took a half an hour's excited discussion before we concluded that it must be Venus, which we had never before seen in an atmosphere that was entirely clear.

To my chagrin I was never as good a skier as I had been a sprinter, but the physical exhilaration, the complete change of ambience and the inevitable edge of danger remained irresistible until I was 80.

One of the pleasantest occasions in the Riesengebirge was on the eve of the New Year, when we would have club races. These were the classical combination of cross-country and ski-jumping, with different tests for the different age-groups. It was a local event, and the tiny neighbourhood children joined in, although some of them were too young to know what a competition was. So they would ski down the hill hand-in-hand, and each receive a bar of chocolate.

Then there was the midnight jumping which usually turned into a wild occasion. Traditionally there would be a blizzard blowing and we would be slightly intoxicated after the New Year's festivities. There would be torches either side of the jump, and it was not unheard of for us to jump directly into the bar.

I agree absolutely with Sir Arnold Lunn, the pioneer of skiing, when he wrote of the contrast between what skiing meant to us and what it means to the contemporary skier: 'It was not only for the joy of the run down that we climbed', he wrote, 'but also for the austere fascination of the undesecrated mountain shrines in winter. It is the multiplication of ski-lifts, unknown in my youth, which has made absolute for most skiers, the divorce between mountaineering and skiing.'

It was indirectly as a result of skiing that I thought of my first poem. I would have been 15 or 16 and I was much moved by the solitude of the solo skier. Also there was something rhythmically seductive about the stamping of my boots as I climbed the hill; this became the metre of the poem. I never wrote it down and it has not survived, which may be just as well! The other poem I recall from this period was of an entirely different nature. I had a friend who was an enthusiastic Dadaist and I found his surreal obsessions utterly ridiculous. To prove it I decided to write my own Dada poem. That too has not survived, although it started: 'Candelabra Orange . . .'

At that time I did not realise the extent to which my attitude to nature was attributable to the influence of the Romantic period in European painting and poetry. I met some people, more mature than I, who preferred towns to mountains, and civilised landscapes such as Mediterranean vineyards and farms to the wild and empty spaces I so much enjoyed. But how to reconcile such romanticism with the analytical objectivity necessary to the naturalist? I concluded that it was not absolutely necessary to be consistent; it was quite possible to admire the moon and its eerie effect on the landscape and human behaviour, while interesting myself in the technicalities of moon rockets and lunar exploration. Broadening the argument, it is perfectly possible to enjoy anthropomorphic poetry in which the landscape is peopled with wood-nymphs and trolls and fairies, while conducting scientific analysis into that same landscape. To describe a coniferous wood as 'taciturn' or a glacier as 'menacing' has as much validity as biological or geological experiments; only one should not confuse the two approaches.

The mountains have always been very special to me, which is why I was so deeply hurt – so *personally* offended – by the way in which even mountaineering became tainted with Fascism when the German and Austrian Alpine Association introduced the Aryan principle into its organisation.

I was more shielded than many of my less fortunate colleagues from the worst excesses of the Nazis. But the rampant anti-Semitism in the Austrian and German universities made it impossible for me to consider the few academic offers made by those who did not know how racially unsuitable I was. The offers came from Vienna and elsewhere and, since I was extremely happy in Prague, I suffered no great loss. For many years German Prague remained an oasis of sanity and a safe house for refugees from persecution.

Not only was I protected from the excesses of Nazism, I was even embarrassed by the efforts made on my behalf by well-meaning colleagues to get exemptions for me. It took time to appreciate the enormity of what was happening elsewhere. Like millions of others I had not read *Mein Kampf*. What I had been told about its content seemed too absurd to merit serious study. I had nothing in common with the caricatured Jew; indeed I identified more strongly with the innocent young Siegfried figures battling single-handedly against the powers of darkness.

Czechoslovakia was such a curious hybrid that I did not in all conscience feel called upon to defend it too vigorously from German imperialist ambitions. I had never been able to justify the separation of the rump of Austria from the main body of Germany, and was not offended by the Anschluss which the Austrians welcomed with such enthusiasm. But this was a very different matter from the unification of two Fascist regimes, and, when the Nazi armies marched into Austria, I suffered the only breakdown of my life, retiring to bed and staying there in a morass of depression and inactivity. After two days I had decided what my response should be, and, getting out of bed, began to plan actively for my future in another country.

The conclusions which I eventually reached were that Fascist repression and terror can recur at almost any time and in almost any place, and produce their evil-smelling blooms most fruitfully if social and political conditions are favourable. It is less to do with nationality than with psychology.

In wartime England I was to find that the propaganda was more virulently anti-German than anti-Fascist. The only good German, people said, was a dead German; Fascism was just a German phenomenon. My conclusions were very different. Having been considered a Jew by the Germans, and a German by the Czech authorities, I could not be persuaded that I should renounce that German part of my personality, which was so very much more developed than my Judaism, always so faint and remote.

For these reasons I found it hard utterly to condemn those of my colleagues who joined the Nazis for reasons of personal advancement. In my case the temptation did not exist. They would not have had me. And so it is difficult to know how I might have behaved had I not had Jewish genes. For me that part of the Lord's Prayer: 'Lead us not into temptation' has always had a particular poignancy.

Having decided to make a new life for myself and my family in another country, the question arose as to which. Sectarianism and prejudice were to drive me out of Czechoslovakia. I needed a country where, belonging to no group or faction, I would be a stranger to everyone and free to choose my own allegiances. Some of my colleagues who had taken the same brave decision as myself favoured Montreal, where the reputation of McGill University was, and remains, high. But in Montreal the conflict between French and English speakers would remind me of Prague, and I rejected that option. Twenty years later Quebec nationalism was to make life uncomfortable for those who had settled in Montreal.

For me the choice was none too difficult. I had already visited England, and read many books on the country. England would be my home and the home of my family. The wisdom of that decision will become apparent in later chapters.

3

Marriage and Exile

In the spring of 1926 Gyula (Julius) John, my mother's brother, invited me to spend some of the summer vacation in Beočin, a village near the south bank of the Danube, between Novisad, also known as Ujvidek or Neusatz, and Belgrade, where he was one of the directors of a cement factory. I was to travel there in the company of Edith, his 15-year-old daughter, who had been at school with my sister Mizzi and who had been staying with us in Prague, her parents being divorced.

But this was not my first visit to Hungary. As a small boy I had been invited by a friend of my mother in the summer of 1916 to stay on a huge estate, Puszta Kengyel, near the town of Szolnok, and that first visit was very much on my mind. I can still recall our arrival in Budapest, where we were to stay overnight. It was evening; the sun was setting and the red and green signal lights flashed past the window as our train approached the station. To me this was a real metropolis, far more exciting than Vienna, where we had changed trains and which had appeared listless and dead. Irma Montagh, who together ith Arpad, her husband, owned the estate, took us in a Mercedes to the elegant Hungaria Hotel. One could not have guessed that the country had already been at war for two or three years. Partly as a result of the English blockade there had been little food in Prague, but there was still plenty in Hungary.

Next morning we arrived at the estate. The house had been built in the style of the region, around three courtyards set in a garden, as yet immature. It was unassuming but it was known as a castle (*kastely*). Irma, the chatelaine, was a formidable matron, blonde, buxom and domineering; we disliked each other on sight, but I got on famously with Arpad, her huge, clean-shaven husband, who moved with the slow deliberation of the countryman. His German was basic and our conversations were limited, but most mornings he would drive me around his estate in a gig, to which he had harnessed two temperamental horses. Holding the reins and the whip gave a town boy an exhilarating experience of power and control.

Vast areas of sunflowers, tobacco and wheat glistened gold in the sunshine. Once we stopped beside an enormous field of stubble to watch a steam engine, imported from England before the war, pulling a plough attached to a cable. We drove on under a pale blue sky, in which larks hovered, until we came to the estate belonging to Montagh's brother, another huge and friendly man.

Dinner in the castle was a formal affair, with family and guests seated at a long table in hierarchical order. I was the youngest and at the 'low' end. Two white-gloved domestics served the food from the top and when there were many guests the plates would be removed before I, who had been served last, had a chance to finish. My noisy protests did little to endear me to the chatelaine. And yet she was most concerned that I should put on weight, and every second evening the family would take me to a huge barn and put me on the scales used to weigh out the corn. Irma would be most indignant to find that I was as skinny as ever, but Arpad would take me stealthily aside and fill my pockets with coins. As I continued to lose weight the ballast became ever heavier. Discovery and disgrace were imminent when history came to our rescue. Romania declared war on Austria-Hungary and my mother and I were advised to go home at once.

So now, a decade later, my cousin Edith and I arrived at the railway station of Novisad in the early hours of St Peter's and Paul's day. The war had been lost, the monarchy dismembered, the town was no longer Hungarian, but a part of the new kingdom of Yugoslavia. Our porter did not speak Magyar but Serb. Yet something of the old order remained.

Edith's father was at the station to meet us, along with his senior fellow director, Ignaz Rosenberg, a tall, fair man with a straw hat and an umbrella. Unknown to us he had joined our train at Budapest the previous evening. And unknown to me he was the father of my future bride. We transferred to the small branch-line train, which crossed the Danube and took us to the hill fortress of Petrovaradin (Peterwardein) and thence via the Fruška Gora, a little mountain range, to our destination, Beočin. But before the train started I disgraced myself; trying to lift my cousin's trunk onto the rack, I broke the compartment window. My uncle, who had to pay for the damage, was clearly unamused, but Mr Rosenberg enjoyed telling the story to his children. I think that my reputation as a super-intellectual which my grandmother had been assiduously spreading was somewhat dispelled by this accident.

At Beočin the smoke from the factory circled imposingly under the cliffs of the quarry and the air vibrated with the rumble of machinery. Coaches awaited us, two sleek browns for us, and two monumental Lippizaner greys for Mr Rosenberg. His coachman, Janos Bacsi (Uncle John), wore a bowler hat and sported a grey beard, like the Emperor Franz Josef. We were to become great friends.

In freshly pressed trousers, a new shirt, and wearing a tie, for the first and last time that summer, I paid my *Antrittsbesuch*, or first call at the Villa Rosenberg. Here I was to encounter a family circle unlike anything I had experienced before and to enter a new phase in my life.

I was staying in my uncle's flat, the first floor of a spacious house in the factory precincts, one of four such apartment houses forming an irregular group shaded by huge plane trees. We passed through the courtyard into the dusty road, along the 'colony' where most of the workers lived and from which rose a cacophony of children's voices intermingled with the clucking of poultry and the grunting of pigs, and crossed a bridge to the gates of the villa garden. A vast dog on a long chain rushed out of its little hut, furiously barking, as we appeared. A winding cement road, flanked by fruit trees, took us up to the big house, a single-storey building, flanked on three sides by extensive terraces. There were views of vineyards and wooded hills on the one side of the Danube, upstream and downstream for many miles.

Here I met Mrs Ilona Rosenberg, a stately matron who greeted us in the most friendly way. Two of her three sons were at home, but her husband was at the factory and her daughter, Nussy, Edith's best friend, was having a piano lesson in Novisad. A servant brought us cold drinks, and there was a lengthy conversation in Magyar, of which I understood not a word. After an hour we went back to lunch with uncle and grandmother.

In the summer holidays the children of the factory employees went swimming. Soon after lunch the 'yellow wagon' would collect them from in front of the factory gates, and, pulled by a big, shaggy horse, take them along a narrow gauge track, which led to the harbour. From the harbour the children would be rowed in an ancient boat across the Danube to a beach near Futog, a 'Swabian' village. The trip was only about a mile, but there was a strong current to contend with. When my cousin and I joined this group on the first day, I was greeted with hilarity. My encounter with the railway window had been widely reported. Maybe I was a studious prig from Prague, but I was also clumsy and possibly even human, as Nussy reported to me later.

Ten years earlier I had met Nussy briefly. A little blonde creature who bore no resemblance to the girl sitting next to me in the wagon, full of high spirits, speaking German with an excruciating Magyar accent, teasing me, radiant. It was love at first sight; it has lasted more than 60 years.

The name Nussy, pronounced Nushi, is derived indirectly, via Anushka and Nushka, from Anna. These diminutives, along with Nushikam, were used as endearments by family and by friends. I shortened the name still further to 'Nush', or even to 'Sh'.

Love at first sight it may have been, but confronted by this princess, I was overcome with shyness and knew myself to be out of my depth. In all but name she was a princess; the only daughter of the paternal head of the factory, living in a huge house, tended by servants, gardeners, coachmen, and even at night by an armed bodyguard. He it was who in later years would disturb our sleep with his snoring and who was dismissed after a drunken night during which he discharged his rifle to the great excitement of the huge mongrel watch-dog.

The garden was stocked with apricot trees. Ducks and geese fed on mulberries; mushrooms grew in a cellar. Villagers, artisans and sometimes pedlars climbed up the road from the village, as well as carts bearing drinking water, ice from the Danube to be stored in man-made caves, and beech-wood from the hills to feed an ingenious but highly temperamental central heating system which on windy days only heated one side of the house. The artisans from the factory could be relied upon for any repairs, and their wives and daughters, who cherished working in 'the house', were only too happy to offer occasional help in the kitchen or with the children.

The salaried employees of the factory and the foremen occupied houses of different styles, sizes and ages in a sort of communal garden landscaped around the works, while the mass of workers and their families lived in a cantonment a few minutes walk away. They were Serbs, Croats, Magyars, Germans from Serbia, Slovaks or Czechs; yet for most of the time, so long as outside events did not interfere, they lived together without much friction.

Every family had an allotment, on which it grew vegetables, fruit and sometimes flowers, and where they kept poultry and a pig or two. Groceries were bought and sold in a co-operative shop, and medical care was supplied by the doctor from the works and a couple of nurses. Wages were low but considerably higher than for labourers on the neighbouring farms.

The hierarchy in the works exemplified the historical changes which had affected the region during the preceding century. The original small cement factory had been started by a family of Budapest Jews at a time when German was still the administrative language in Hungary, and German was still the internal language of the big combine 80 years later. The descendants of the original family were still the absentee owners at the time of which I am writing. The technicians were Jews, Hungarians and Germans as they had always been, though younger Serbs and Croats had started to fill the intermediate grades.

The site of the factory was particularly attractive. It lay between a range of hills of limestone and chalk, suitable for cement manufacture, and the Danube, which provided cheap transport not only for the cement but also for coal which was delivered upstream from a mine belonging to the same owners. Thus, as long as the monarchy lasted, Budapest, Vienna and other smaller towns could be directly supplied from the local harbour. And when the Hapsburg Empire crumbled in 1918, Belgrade, the growing Yugoslav capital, just 80 miles away, provided the new market. The only serious complications arose from the redrawing of borders. The central administration remained in Budapest with one 'daughter' factory in true rump Hungary. Beočin, the original factory, and several other works found themselves in Yugoslavia, with others in Czechoslovakia, Austria and Romania. A holding company had to be set up in Switzerland to deal with the complicated nationality problems. Inevitably after the Second World War all the factories in the Communist sector were appropriated, although the Beočin tradition lives on with cement factories in Brazil and East Africa and a port for transporting the stuff in India. But when I visited Beočin the factory was still a quasi-autonomous enclave in the new Yugoslovia, and, thanks to its wealth, independent of outside pressures. Employment, schooling, medical care and social and cultural life were all locally organised, and only the post-office, the police, and the railway station were state-administered. Visas for foreigners like myself, permits and suchlike red-tape were in the hands of a special employee, who took over the role of a consular official. I never dealt directly with the Yugoslav authorities. It was a fedual world, a charming anachronism in a fast-changing Europe.

Every morning Janos brought the Lippizaners, apple-grey with pink nostrils, and harnessed to a brougham, to the front of the house and on the stroke of eight the 'King' mounted his carriage and, sitting erect, walking-stick in hand, was driven to his office in the factory.

Princesses did not go to school, so Nussy was taught by private tutors, a titled Russian lady for French, an aged pupil of Liszt for piano. She wore elegant clothes bought in Budapest, she read novels and poetry in three languages. Interested in gossip, her high spirits concealed an innocent serenity. What a contrast to me, poor, scruffy, puritanical, and up to this moment in my life, in love only with ideas.

When I remember our courtship I see a boat moored to a small wooden pier while we waded through the muddy, yellow-brown water into the shadow of some poplars. There we would leave our baskets of food and drink and change into our swimming costumes. Staying within the shadow of the bank we would let ourselves be carried a mile or so downstream to a low island which Nussy told me had not been there the previous summer. It was just a sandbank without the willows and poplars that characterised older islands. We were quite alone in the middle of the Danube. The water was warm and the sun hot. An occasional fishing boat drifted past. Storks circled in the sky.

I did not realise on the day of our first swim that I had entered an enchanted world, almost a medieval fairy-tale. I had fallen in love with a princess, lively, elegant and affectionate, the beloved only daughter with three good-hearted but mischievous brothers. At this time they were home for the holidays from their various colleges. After my first visit to Beočin in 1926 I came every year. Nussy and I were married in 1932 in the Old Town Hall in Prague. Peter was born in Prague in 1933 and George in Beočin two years later. Elsa was born in England 10 years after George.

I've always been interested in rivers. The Moldau flows through my earliest memories, rafts shooting through sluices, ice-floes under the old bridge, gulls crying overhead while I swam under the old castle of Visegrad. As an adolescent, I would fall asleep to the sound of the water tumbling over the New Town Weir. It was natural therefore that my doctoral thesis should deal with the riverbed fauna of the Moldau within Prague. This was an early ecological study, long before ecology became fashionable and politically useful. I measured the physical and chemical properties of the water in six localities and analysed the microscopic animals living in and above the mud. Like so much in this book, my thesis refers to a vanished world. The Moldau has been dammed upstream from Prague and the cold water released from the artificial lakes together with effluent purification and industrial pollution has profoundly altered the conditions of life on the river bottom.

My interest in these matters led to my being put in charge of the practical side of the hydrobiological studies, which my old and revered teacher, Professor Carl Cori, offered the Prague students each summer term. In later years Nussy and I were to explore the varied and ever-changing habitats of the untamed Danube in a folding canoe; the open river, the narrow canals, the stagnant side arms, the drying pools, the sunlit places and the shaded creeks, the water fowl and the geese and ducks from nearby villages.

One of my reasons for not totally immersing myself in biological studies of the Danube was that the continental summer climate of the region provided ideal conditions for investigating the behaviour of bees and in particular their sense of time. I had been greatly impressed by recent studies around this subject, notably a lecture by von Frisch, and I took the opportunity to study the existence of an internal clock for bees, which we have come to call the circadian rhythm. I was able to confirm that by feeding syrup to a number of bees for an hour, they would on the next day visit the feeding site perfunctorily during the same hour. It was also possible to train the same bees to visit two different sites at different hours of the day. Thus one could see why they were able to visit flowers which open at different times. By chilling the bees or keeping them in a CO_2 atmosphere I could delay the hour of their visit, from which I deduced that their urge to forage was indeed controlled by an internal, metabolic mechanism, which acted like an alarm clock to remind them to feed at a particular time, but which, like a clock, could be made to run slow.

This kind of behavioural study is much improved when individual bees can be identified. Von Frisch had devised a system of applying a code of dots to the thorax and abdomen of bees. Sometimes I copied him, at other times it was sufficient simply to daub bees' thoraxes with different colours, red, green, yellow etc. My technique of daubing them without disturbing them while they were sucking syrup from a petri dish made a deep impression on the man who owned them, a jovial schoolmaster, who was fascinated to see what 'the biologist from the university' was doing with his beloved bees. Since he spoke only Hungarian and Serb, we had serious problems of communication, and I could never explain satisfactorily to him what it was that I was after.

One day red daubed bees appeared in large numbers at the feeding dish, but not only in the morning as I had anticipated. There they were again in the late afternoon, and I observed that one or two of them had a little red paint on their wing, which looked like none of my doing. I caught and counted all the red bees. There were 53, although I had only marked 25. My friend had clearly been doing some research on his own!

My bee observations were carried out in the garden belonging to Nussy's parents; it surrounded their villa on the hill. A short walk away were some stables, abandoned for the most part, and one of these stables I converted into an office cum laboratory, which stood ready for me, whenever I arrived from Prague. Next to this improvised laboratory was a house inhabited by a very old retainer, who had lived on his own since his wife's death, revelling in the company of a collection of old and sick animals, a dog, a goat, and for several summers a stork, which he had found with a broken wing on the shore of the Danube. He knew a great deal about animal behaviour.

The sociology of insects has always fascinated people, even in the most primitive times. More recently political dogma has insisted either that analogies with human behaviour can be drawn from the behaviour of ants, bees and wasps or that no such comparisons are valid under any circumstances. My view is that insect behaviour may provide quite valuable insights into certain features of human society.

One of the difficulties about observing animals is to decide whether what appears to be co-ordinated behaviour may not just be the parallel reaction of many individuals to the same stimuli, as it might be the attraction of a prey or the incidence of the sun's rays. I have watched numerous insect societies both experimentally and in natural surroundings. The behaviour of swarming midges, for example, is instructive and paradoxical. A midge or mosquito may dance up and down in a column over some hot stone or tree and then, separated from its fellows, perform a similar dance above another heat-radiating object, one's hand, perhaps, or one's bare body. These dancing swarms occur in vast agglomerations. I remember an evening on a bluff overlooking a lake in western Canada, when every poplar tree was crowned with a huge black column of thousands of these insects visible against the darkening sky as far as the eye could see. And each individual insect could be deflected in the manner I have just described. It seems that the dance is an individual activity stimulated probably by the sexual state of the swarming males and females; but the hot air rising from the trees brings together both sexes into a dance which ends with a mating ritual.

The mass phenomena of tropical insects are even more impressive. Once, walking by night through the forest in West Africa, I heard a very slight rustling and felt small objects falling on me. I was in fact being rained upon by a variety of dead insects and debris from the trees above me. Closer inspection revealed that there were millions of ants foraging in the branches and foliage, killing and jettisoning everything and anything that lived, beetles, orthopters, butterflies and even, I have been told although I have not observed it, small birds. Other members of the ant colony collect the remains and carry them to their subterranean nests. In a single night areas comprising several hectares can be denuded of all life. So thorough are the ants that after a while the huge colony will go on the march and start a new nesting site half a mile away, and that too will be devastated.

During the day one sees nothing of all this, of course. The ants are in the undergrowth, marching purposefully hither and thither, not in the trees. On several occasions I have seen these marches crossing a small rivulet where the bridge was formed by living ants which clung together so that others could cross on their backs over the water. Is this co-operation the effect of some parallel reaction to similar impulses and stimuli? Experiments have been inconclusive, serving only to reinforce the prejudices of the various experimenters.

No sign of co-operation was discernible during the nuptial flights of termites which I witnessed in West Africa. Millions would swarm around the lights of the swimming pool and the wings and the corpses of the victims of the sexual frenzy would pile up around the pool and even on the surface of the water a foot or more high. I do not think that in this case the individuals paid the slightest attention to which of the company had or had not mated before, but the corpses of the dead or dying would be collected in buckets and taken home by humans to be fried and eaten.

At an early stage in my scientific development I determined that nothing should be allowed to stand in the way of biological experimentation, so long as it was clearly conceived and could be seen to be of some practical use. I volunteered for, and was one of five students selected to participate in, the advanced course of physiology run by Professor H. H. Kahn. He insisted that we should be meticulous in our techniques and that we should always take great care in our use of anaesthetics; I never formed the impression that the dogs or cats on which we operated suffered acute pain. However, I did find it repugnant to discard as a corpse a cat which a couple of hours earlier had purred and rubbed itself against my shin, or a dog which had jumped up to greet me. I did not and do not object to this kind of experimentation but I felt that I should leave it to those who enjoy it more.

But I do object strongly to amateurish, useless or unnecessary vivisection as practised in many countries, and in several laboratories I have watched colleagues doing horrific things. My aversion to intrusive animal experimentation naturally led me in two different directions: ethology, the study of animal behaviour in natural or manipulated surroundings, and experimentation with humans. In both areas I have been accused of cruel and even dangerous practices, although I have always been careful to avoid such charges. My book, *100 Simple Experiments with Insects*, was attacked for teaching children to mutilate insects, and the taste testing for phenylthiourea (PTC) was pilloried as a danger to children. This substance tastes very bitter to some people whereas others find it completely tasteless, which is a genetical trait. Testing for this difference has been performed routinely in schools using methods developed by Harris and myself. Over 10,000 people have been tested without – so far as I know – any untoward effects. Over-vigilance can easily become counter-productive.

Some really dangerous and unpleasant experiments are necessary. One example is the high-pressure research for determining the best conditions for escaping from sunken submarines, described later in this book. A reliable rule in such cases is never to ask others to do or to experience what you have not yourself already done or experienced.

Among the marine biological stations I visited the most important was Heligoland. I spent six weeks there participating in the courses and another six weeks employed by the Prussian government to investigate the breeding of oysters.

The North Sea oyster had been in decline for some time. The larvae did not settle on the old oyster shells or on the oyster grounds; that much was known but nobody could explain the phenomenon. I was as unsuccessful as the rest. It was eventually discovered that the cause was a deficiency in copper in the sea water.

The courses at the Heligoland station were interesting in themselves, but of even more interest to me was the opportunity to meet a wide circle of biologists, from as far away as India and Japan. Some of the time I spent with my old professor-in-chief, Carl Cori, from Prague, and we enjoyed long evening walks on the cliffs while discussing all sorts of matters, from biology to politics. In the old Austria-Hungary he had been in charge of a marine biology station in Trieste, disbanded by the Italians in 1918. He was not only a graduate in zoology and medicine, but also a certified sea-captain with a vast knowledge of marine affairs. At heart he was still a Hapsburg monarchist who had been disappointed with the achievements of the new order, but he was a very mild man, and any kind of radical violence would have been anathema to him.

There were other colleagues too from Arthur Biedl's Department of Experimental Biology in Prague. One of them was young and reckless, both in the nature of his experiments and in his personal relationships. I collaborated with him on some large-scale slaughtering of plaice and other fish to explore their lack of certain internal organs, experiments which proved futile and of which I am now heartily ashamed. Dr Reis, a milder character, was chiefly concerned with avoiding the journeys on the research vessels. I vividly recall him during the course of a vicious gale, praying for deliverance, behaviour which strongly contrasted with his traditional and powerfully-held atheism.

There was an ornithological station on the island and I struck up an acquaintance with some of the bird-watchers, walking along the cliff-top with them, binoculars in hand. But I found them irritating. They seemed only interested in the species or sub-species and never mentioned the genus, so that, as a zoologist, I had little idea of what they were talking about.

There were several grand old men stationed there. There was Albrecht Bitte, for example, the famous physiologist and father of the atomic physicist; there was Escherich, the leading forestry scientist in Germany and the man who gave his name to the best known bacterium, *Escherichia*.

I lived in the cottage belonging to a fisherman called Heinrich, a charming elderly man with a motherly wife, and both of them looked after me delightfully. But the son of the house had become infected with the Nazi bug and I was to listen more than once to heated family arguments, particularly after one of the elections in which the Nazis made considerable gains. I remember too Dr von Hertling, a descendant of one of the Bismarck liberals, being utterly dejected as the results were announced; but he too was to become a functionary of the Nazis.

On the beach children built sand-castles, but there were two competing German flags in evidence, the old imperial colours of black, white and red, and the black, red and yellow of the Weimar Republic. The proportion was about two for Wilhelm to every one for the Republic. The Swastika was not much in evidence but to an outsider such as myself the confusion between jingoistic nationalism and National Socialism was ominously evident.

One of the old-fashioned romantics, dreaming of an age gone by, of chivalry and moral purity, was Dr Emm, one of our marine biologists, but greatly interested in falconry too. One evening we were walking along the cliff-top when Dr Emm suddenly called out 'Astur!', a name he had given to a female sparrow-hawk which had escaped, and to the astonishment of both of us, one of the nearby sparrow-hawks flew down and settled on Dr Emm's outstretched hand. A magic moment.

The main result of my weeks of research on the island was the discovery that some larvae previously recorded as such, in fact belonged to a species taxonomically quite far removed. Whether or not the entries in the plankton records of Heligoland were altered, I was certainly none too popular when I told my colleagues of my discovery.

There were many severe gales on Heligoland that year. The harbour piers were completely unapproachable and the dunes were flooded, so we would walk on the upper island. Together with an elderly lady biologist from Leipzig and a young one from Berlin, I undertook an expedition to Silt, one of the East Friesian group. The landscape was beautiful, and I observed for the first time decoy ducks on the ponds to lure wild ducks to their destruction. The mood amongst the Silt inhabitants was tense, and the summer guests were quite blatantly and unpleasantly anti-Semitic. I realised then that the Nazis would prevail in Germany and that I should have no professional career there.

Besides Heligoland I also worked at marine stations at Villefranche-sur-Mer and Varna. Villefranche had been an imperialist Russian research establishment; after the Revolution it was kept going partly by the Czech government, which rented a couple of work benches and put them at the disposal of Czech researchers. I was lucky enough to win one of the working scholarships.

The station was an old prison situated on the coast. One could still see the rings in the walls to which prisoners had been chained. I remember most vividly an old fisherman called Hyacinth who was improbably terrified of bad weather, and whenever the mistral blew, no matter how gently, he would announce that it was 'très mauvais' and he would on no account venture out to fish or catch plankton. Although there was no formal instruction the library was extremely useful. Life was simple. I cooked, very modestly, for myself, finding the local French cooking not particularly attractive. Once I thought I could prepare a *Sepia* and boiled it. However, I must have done something wrong because it was not only inedible but when one threw it to the floor it bounced back like a tennis ball.

Among interesting visitors to Villefranche were Paul Weiss, who was to become scientific adviser to President Eisenhower, and von Brunn, the biographer of Mendel, who used to go out collecting alpine plants with a pupil. On one or two occasions I was invited to accompany them, and learnt a great deal about plant ecology. Poor Hugo was greatly agitated by the anti-Semitism and, being of Jewish origins but married to a German gentile, began to have private doubts about his marriage and children.

The marine biological station at Varna, on the Black Sea in Bulgaria, was – and probably still is – understaffed and under-equipped. Our living quarters were primitive and, while my friends were swimming and sunbathing, I took a few days off to study the flora and fauna of the region, but there was little of interest. The director of the station suggested that we might like to take a trip across the bay in search of the bones of marine tortoises which were to be found amongst the dunes. He had summoned some cadets from the Royal Bulgarian Naval Academy to row us to the site. At one point the monotony of the coastline was broken by what appeared to be a huge park, and I asked the cadets to moor there and let us explore. They seemed reluctant to do so, but I insisted. No sooner had we landed than a sentry appeared with a fixed bayonet; we were under arrest. We had dared to set foot, it seemed, on the garden of the royal palace with the royal family in attendance. Dr Friedl Pick, my old friend from Prague who had introduced me to the pleasures of palaeontology explained in French to an officer that we were famous international scientists, and that we had been transported there by cadets of the King's own Naval Academy. In order to verify that we were whom we claimed to be, the officer summoned his head gardener and examined Dr Schwartz, Pro-fessor of Botany in Jerusalem and Dean of the Science Faculty, in the names of the flowers in the royal garden. There were complications because the botanical names are not always the names that the horticulturalists use, but in the end the elderly gardener did confirm

42

that Dr Schwartz knew quite a bit about plants, and we were allowed to leave. All these diplomatic negotiations had taken place with one side in full uniform, the other in bathing trunks.

Poor Dr Pick! Despite my warnings he had not applied any anti-sunshine lotion and, particularly vulnerable as a result of his fair complexion, he was dreadfully sunburnt. Having applied some ointment he went again to the beach. Consequently his burnt skin and the analgesic ointment were covered in sand, so that he looked not unlike a cod fillet or a wiener schnitzel which had been coated in breadcrumbs! We applied olive oil to his skin and some hot water to gently wash away the sand, but for the rest of our stay he kept well out of the sun.

The uncanny limbo in which we lived after Hitler's accession to power in Germany had curious consequences. During the winters I used to ski in the Giant Mountains, which then formed the border between Germany and Czechoslovakia, now between Poland and Czechoslovakia. The border was mostly unmarked and such frontier stones as there were were buried in snow, so that one was never sure whether one was in the Democratic Republic or in Nazi Germany. This gave a certain piquancy to one's wanderings in blizzards and one's encounters with strangers and friends, often no clearer than oneself about the local geography.

It has always been an interesting border. When it divided Austria and Russia smugglers would cross in either direction as the need arose. Nor was it only money and gold which were transported, but saccharine, taxed in Austria but not in Germany, or cigarettes, or drink. During the great inflation after the First World War, smuggling was a favourite occupation for amateurs as well as professionals. I often met young people in the middle of the night carrying lampstands, a couple of guitars, or even rubber dinghies through the icy darkness.

When it became clear that I could not hope to stay in Prague, I started to look energetically for possibilities elsewhere. While living at my parents-in-law's house in Yugoslavia, I discovered that in Skoplje there was a malaria station, which was the relic of a unit left behind by the German army and staffed since the end of the First World War by the Belgrade Health Ministry. I wrote to the director of the station, and asked whether I could visit Skoplje and learn something about malaria. He readily agreed.

My few weeks in Skoplje were memorable. I learned the rudiments of malariology, and found myself uncommonly popular. At the Czech consulate when it was known that I was studying at the Malaria Institute, several people insisted on talking German to me, which just a few months earlier would have seemed highly improbable. They also suggested that I should buy shares in some Macedonian mines to ensure that the Nazis should not get them all. Most remarkable was the presence of an elderly Viennese baron, whom they addressed with all the courtesy and titles used in the old monarchy whose implacable enemies they had formerly been. I did my best to console them and to reassure them that Czechoslovakia would survive however terrible the next few years might be.

From the windows of my laboratory I could see snow-covered peaks, and was irresistibly tempted. I got the key to a chalet run by the local Alpine club and hired a dragoman, who came equipped with two mules. One weekend evening we set off, ski-sticks and rucksacks festooned around our saddles. It took us several hours to reach the rather sparse snow, and after another hour we came to a decently furnished hut already occupied by two other people. After brewing our tea I noticed that one of them was shivering violently. He explained to me that he was recuperating from influenza and that his doctor had sent him to the mountains to recover. At once I suspected malaria, and gave him some quinine. Within a few hours he was perfectly all right. It amazed me to think that any doctor could have been so mistaken in his diagnosis.

In the evening the dragoman told me the story of his life. He had been born in Slovakia, had served in the old Austrian army, and had been buffeted between various states and organisations all his life. He spoke five languages. His greatest accomplishment, he claimed, was his skill in testing tobacco for an Austrian tobacco monopoly.

The following morning I set off alone climbing towards the peaks. On the sunny side of the slopes there was very little snow but numerous sheep. These, I learned later, were the cause of considerable friction as they were always being driven across the Yugoslav-Albanian border and nobody knew any longer to whom they actually belonged. This was one of those rare occasions when I was to find myself entirely alone in a vast wintry landscape, the only ski-tracks being my own.

The malaria station had an ambulance and from time to time trips would be made to the outlying villages to treat malaria sufferers. One day I was asked to substitute for the regular doctor, who had been invited to a wedding. Although alarmed at my lack of experience and my inability to share a language with the people I would be treating, I was persuaded to go. We made our way to a Muslim community living an isolated existence in the mountains around Skoplje. These hill-inhabitants of Macedonia had managed to avoid being slaughtered by the various marauding armies as they passed down into the plains, but were in a pitiable state, stunted, semi-starved, and suffering from numerous diseases, including malaria. They claimed that they lived in the hills not so much to escape the soldiers as the mosquitoes and to gain the benefit of the 'good air'. Unfortunately the fields they tilled were several kilometres away down in the plains.

In a room in the school was a nurse, an old technician and myself. Our clients formed two lines, men and women. When each patient came in, he or she would be asked a few questions, and the technician would take a blood sample, which he would spread on a slide and stain. According to his diagnosis and after a few more questions the nurse would dispense some quinine or other anti-malarial pills and the patient would be required to swallow them in our presence. Otherwise, I was told, they would trade them in for money. Peculiar problems arose in the case of the Muslim women, who were deeply veiled and in thick black clothes, so that I could neither examine them nor persuade them to undress. All I could do was ask a few simple questions and get the nurse to interpret the answers for me. But the results were valuable. Between late autumn and early summer new infections could not occur in Macedonia due to the low tempertures. This enabled me to compare the efficacy of quinine treatment with the medication of the new anti-malarials which had been developed in Germany. The rationale was that patients would return if the treatment had not been successful, but would not return if they had suffered no further attacks (possibly in a few cases because they had died). But my results showed that indeed the new anti-malarials were more effective than the old quinine.

My Skoplje interlude at an end, I had to plan for the future and to consider in which country that future might be. During the 20 years of the first Czechoslovak Republic the fragmentation of the people of Prague had increased. The differences between the half-dozen Czech parties had sharpened and amongst the Germans the ever-increasing pressures of Nazism deepened the chasm between Aryans and non-Aryans. Outsiders were steadily reinforcing the latent anti-Semitism, until for many Zionism or Communism or both, appeared to be the only solutions to a desperate problem. The terrifying disintegration of social coherence affected my schoolmates, my colleagues and my friends. Those I had believed to be pacifists, or, at least, non-political, became members of the SS, Marxist agitators, Zionist organisers, even Adventists or diabolists. Some just sat and hoped that the trouble would blow over, but to most of us it became ever clearer that Prague was no longer an acceptable home. I reached this conclusion on the day Hitler marched into Vienna. I had my one and only breakdown, but when, two days later, I recovered, the way seemed clear. I had to leave Prague, if possible for England.

4

Wartime England

I had visited England before. In the autumn of 1922, when I was 16, my father encouraged me, although if the decision had been mine alone I should probably have preferred a skiing holiday in the Alps.

I travelled with a group of young Czech members of the YMCA; I was the only German speaker amongst them. My father gave me a £10 note and a return ticket, and, despite spending a week in London and visiting Oxford, Cambridge and Canterbury, I still had enough left to pay the excess on my ticket which would enable me to return home via the Alps. I cannot pretend to have been impressed with my first sight of the English Channel or the white cliffs of Dover, and our camp, sited on the Isle of Sheppey, must have been one of the least attractive places in the United Kingdom.

The camp was run by Oxford and Cambridge students for the YMCA. Most of the English boys there were East Enders, and since I shared a tent with several of them I was way out of my depth. I found it intriguing however. There were three Christian services on Sunday, to which some of the militant atheists amongst the Czechs objected. Asked to sing their own hymns, it transpired that they knew the melodies but not the words so they improvised satirical and slightly pornographic lyrics which they put to the sacred tunes. This was all very well until the visit of the Secretary to the Czech Embassy . . .

The food was unfamiliar, but I thought it excellent. Athletic competitions were organised and, being a useful swimmer and high jumper, I won regularly and was rewarded with a shilling. Not surprisingly the Czechs, who had until then regarded me as an outsider, now hailed me as a great champion. I became friendly with one of the East End kids, who gave me a book. He told me that he was not at all happy with the running of the camp, and felt considerable class resentment. I had been aware of course of the cultural differences between the young people running the place and the inmates. The experience not only taught me a good deal about the British, but it gave me my first insights into the way young Czechs talked and behaved.

I suppose that this early visit to Britain ensured that when the time came to leave Prague, I would make England my home. Decisions were taken, arrangements made, farewells concluded.

Having crossed the Czechoslovak-Hungarian border on foot, as the direct train service had been interrupted, Nussy and I spent a night in a hotel in Budapest, talking to old friends, whom we should never see again. Next day, 23 December 1938, we arrived at my wife's family home in Yugoslavia. It was early morning. Nothing had apparently changed there; when we had left for Prague a few months before we had left our two little boys with their grandmother, and they had enjoyed themselves in our absence. The presents on Christmas Eve were more plentiful than ever. On New Year's Eve there was a sumptuous party in my brother-in-law's house in Belgrade. During the drive back, through gently falling snow, Nussy and I fell silent. We both felt that this was the end of an epoch – at least for us. The thought occurred to me that we had just re-enacted a scene from some age-old play: a ball in a French or Russian castle at the start of some revolution perhaps. All I said was: 'Well, that's the last time.'

Late in the evening on New Year's Day, I put on my skis and set out for the hills. Plenty of snow had fallen and at first I felt relieved and even exhilarated, but the snow melted to slush, and, when it began to rain, I returned, slaloming incongruously and disconsolately through dripping vineyards.

After a depressing week of waiting, I at last received the message from London, confirming that I had an excellent chance of being given one of the grants that had been set up to help refugee scholars. Other good news was that I could also enjoy hospitality set aside for those like myself who could expect no support from Jewish or Socialist organisations. I packed my bag and left for England via Italy and France. I did not look out of the train. I thought it probable that I would never see a blue lake or a white mountain again.

I had useful introductions in London, to a Liberal Member of Parliament, to the Duchess of Atholl, who knew my mother from meetings of the International League for Peace and Freedom, and to the proto-zoologists of the London School of Hygiene and Tropical Medicine. I was thankful that, with these useful contacts, I was greeted with no bureaucratic problems when I passed through immigration at Folkestone.

The Strand Palace Hotel struck me as considerably less grand than its name, but it was there that, like so many refugees, I spent my first night. Upon arrival I had telephoned John and Jean Garrick, friends in Hampstead Garden Suburb, who suggested that I should at once leave the Strand Palace and move in with them. A quick computation reassured me that I had just enough money for a night at the hotel, and either dinner or a telephone conversation with Nussy. I settled for the conversation and a cup of coffee.

John and Jean were middle-aged actors, semi-retired and living modestly in an idyllic small house and garden. John painted botanical and other still-life subjects. Jean was an active part of the Hampstead cultural set-up. They put me up in their son's room, for he had left home a year earlier. They were astonishingly kind, the weather was sunny and warm for January, and, with little time to brood or read the threatening reports in the papers, I was wonderfully happy. I was busy trying to establish myself, to resume my work, to make the necessary arrangements for my family to join me and, with Jean's help, to explore the cultural life of Hampstead Garden Suburb and the West End. I realised how much catching up I had to do when I attended a Hampstead lecture about a family called the Brontes, of whom I had never heard and who sounded to my mind rather peculiar.

More interesting were the visits to the local Everyman Theatre which presented plays about contemporary issues. But I felt completely at home when Jean took me to see a West End production of *A Midsummer Night's Dream*. The red and gold auditorium, the crystal chandeliers, the plush curtain, the animated hum of the public, the tuning-up of the orchestra, all this was so familiar that for a moment or two I forgot where I was. It was not until everybody stood up to greet the opening bars of the National Anthem that I woke up to the realisation that I was a long way from home. It also struck me that the melody of 'God Save the King' had once been used to applaud the Kaiser.

But soon enough Mendelssohn's music, Shakespeare's gaiety and the liveliness of the acting, restored the illusion that nothing much in the world had changed. For a couple of hours or more, England appeared less a place of exile than a country to which I had returned. But after the curtain-calls the actors appeared in front of the curtain to appeal for money for exiled actors, and I remembered that Mendelssohn's music was now proscribed in his native country. Something terrible had happened after all.

My search for a place in the English scientific community was surprisingly easy and short. I was interviewed by a Mr Thorn in an office at Gordon Square and a week later I received a letter from the Society for the Protection of Science and Learning with the welcome news that I had been given a grant of £250 a year. Also enclosed was a letter to the immigration authorities asking them, in the light of this award, to admit my wife and sons to Britain. This I sent off directly to Nussy.

A word about this unique and very English organistion would be appropriate here. Founded, and for the most part funded, by academics outraged by what was happening in Hitler's Germany, it has over several decades helped to rescue hundreds of scholars and scientists from a number of oppressive regimes. Having rescued them, it strives to re-establish them. The contribution of these outcasts to the world's culture has been extraordinary and quite out of proportion to their number. Miss Esther Simpson, tireless secretary and mother to us all, has kept a meticulous register, happily entering every new Nobel Laureate, every Fellow of the Royal Society, every Professor. Some of us, rescued by the Society, were able to help in the rehabilitation of later victims of persecution.

Finding somewhere to work was more difficult. My grant stipulated that I work at some university or research institution, but my first attempt to secure such a post was a failure, and a dismal one. I visited the Zoology Department of a Midlands town. The Professor and his academic colleagues appeared distinctly provincial, were critical of my work and seemed to disapprove of me personally. But they offered me a place, which I declined.

My decision was less rash than it must have appeared to these astonished and possibly offended academics, because the day before I had received news from the bank that Nussy's eldest brother had succeeded in sending me some money which was on deposit for me in Switzerland. If, as Schopenhauer is alleged to have said, 'freedom is a bank account' I could now enjoy a little freedom. I did not have to take the first research post that was offered to me.

An improvement in my circumstances came about through the mediation of Gottfried Fraenkl, an older and much admired colleague from Frankfurt, with whom in more settled days I had enjoyed time both in the laboratory and on the rocky research vessel of the Sorbonne's marine biological station in Roscoff, Brittany. He advised me to write to G.P. ('Gip') Wells, the son of H.G. Wells, at University College. Like me, Gip was a comparative physiologist.

My first visit to University College was to decide the course of the remainder of my life. As I climbed the stairs in the Zoology building, converted from the stables of an old coaching company, I met a surly man in trenchcoat and cloth cap and asked him the whereabouts of Dr Wells's room. He grunted something which I took to mean that I should follow him; on the first floor corridor he grunted something, pointed with his pipe at a door, and disappeared.

I knocked, entered, and introduced myself to the jovial Wells. He was in a laboratory coat, I spruce in my Sunday best, but he received me amiably. I spotted an edition of *Zeitschrift für Vergleichende Physiologie* on Wells's desk. This contained my latest paper. After some discussion he promised that he would recommend to D.M.S. Watson, the head of the department, a former palaeontologist and expert on extinct elephants, that he should offer me a place. I would continue my work on diurnal rhythms (the subject of my article in the journal on his desk). Wells told me that I could expect to hear from Watson and should send him copies of any articles that I might have.

While we were talking, the door opened and the man I had met on the stairs, now without his hat and his coat but still puffing on his pipe, came in. He listened for a while and then left without saying a word. Wells must have noticed my bewilderment because he asked me who I supposed the man was. I said that I fancied him to be an old laboratory factotum, who had come in to take a closer look at an unfamiliar visitor. In my experience of similar institutions indispensable aged servants often enjoy such liberties. Wells laughed.

'That man is Haldane,' he said. I was even more baffled. The

Haldane I knew of, the physiologist, had been dead for some years, and I said so.

'Not J.B.,' said Wells, 'his son, J.B.S. Have you never heard of him?' I said that I had not.

It was not long before I received a friendly letter from Professor Watson, informing the Society that I had been accepted as a researcher in University College. I started at once, resuming my work on the 24-hour periodicity in various functions of an invertebrate, the fruit fly Drosophila, and a vertebrate, the axolotl, a Mexican newt.

Meanwhile I was handed over by the Garricks to another Hampstead household. Basil Hume, a surgeon in St Bartholomew's, had originally offered me hospitality, but his wife had had a car accident just before my arrival in England, which is why I had gone initially to the Garricks. Now the Humes claimed me. It was a very different household. The doctor was only home in the evenings. Mrs Hume, the strict mother of three little girls, was rather less tolerant than the Garricks of my continental ways. I began to feel the pangs of separation from my wife and children, and this contributed to my sensitivity and unhappiness. The diet and the inadequate heating exacerbated the situation.

I would be given a huge breakfast from which I could only recover by walking to the tube station across Hampstead Heath. But the college lunches were insufficient, and supper was usually cocoa and biscuits, fine for little girls but not for me. Probably the Humes never understood that I was sometimes hungry and frequently cold in my room, although a hot water bottle was a welcome novelty. At weekends the girls taught me about English manners in the most innocent and charming way. On Sundays I was taken to Friends Meetings.

Getting Nussy and the boys to England proved to be complicated. The first hurdle was a directive issued by the Yugoslav government that no visa should be granted to a Jew. Before my departure I had been with Nussy to the Yugoslav Consulate in Prague. As a Christian, I received my visa automatically but Nussy was refused. Other considerations apart this meant that she would be unable to return to her place of birth and join our sons there. However, an outburst of rage and a few tears softened the heart of the consular official, who in any case had been unhappy about this Nazi-inspired legislation. In the end Nussy was enabled to enter her homeland on the strength of my christening certificate issued two years before she was born.

After she received my letter containing the document recommending her admission to Britain, she encountered a similar difficulty at the French Consulate in Belgrade. Transit visas could only be issued if the applicant had already obtained an entry visa to Britain; besides which a French visa could be issued only in the home country of the applicant. Nussy, being a Czech citizen, had not needed a British visa and consequently did not have one. Fortunately in due course a secretary was prevailed upon to accept the letter of recommendation in lieu of a visa. On this occasion it was the flirtatiousness of one of Nussy's friends which overcame the bureaucrats. Two days after this happy outcome Hitler's army entered Prague. Had Nussy been forced to return there to get her visa she would probably never have escaped.

I received a telegram announcing Nussy's arrival with the children at Dover on the Ides of March, 1939. I had no idea by which route they would arrive, and in Dover I bought an evening paper which carried the news that the German army was in Prague. I sat on the cliffs with my paper and wondered whether the boat which was due in two hours time would bring my family to me. Time passed very slowly. When they finally emerged from the customs shed, I discovered that they did not yet know what had taken place in Prague. I gave them the details over a cup of tea on the boat-train.

Now that I had a research position in London, a guaranteed income from my grant and the money from Switzerland in reserve, I could afford the £8 a month it cost to rent a small house in a cul-de-sac in Hampstead Garden Suburb. Our furniture and personal effects had reached me from Prague – though rather waterlogged they were none the less welcome – and the only items that were missing were a few books, six pairs of skis, an ice axe, some ropes and a rubber dinghy. Morna Coldstream, a friend of Nussy's from her finishing school in Paris had helped me furnish the little house and unpack the trunks. It was crowded. The Bosendorfer grand piano occupied half the space in the sitting-room, and a small sideboard had to be put on top of a larger one. But we did have water, gas, electricity, coal in the bunker and a little food in the larder. What more should we need? After supper with the Humes we moved to Hampstead Garden Suburb.

The neighbourhood was mainly composed of middle-class couples with small children. Everyone was friendly and helpful. Some even apologised that they had 'let Czechoslovakia down'.

On the first morning after Nussy's arrival there were three milk deliveries. Every time we opened the door there seemed to be two pints of milk standing there. It transpired that three different dairies were serving the district, the green, the blue and the red; we stopped the green and the blue. After the third milk delivery of the morning, a salesman called and took our order for groceries. The butter, eggs and bacon which he later brought were of the finest quality, all English, and costing half as much again as the foreign produce which was also available. It took us a while to become alert to these discrepancies.

We were lucky and we knew it. We had our own house – albeit rented – with our own things, and some less fortunate refugees were frequent visitors. But the drop in our standard of living was severe, especially for Nussy. For the first time in her life she had no cook, no maid, no hairdresser or beauty salon, no pampering at all in fact.

Peter had been six in January and after Easter he would need to go to school. We enrolled him in the suburban primary. Like his younger brother George, he spoke German. When they arrived in England, neither of them spoke a word of English; when Peter entered school he spoke hardly any. He arrived home after his second or third day at school in tears with black stripes on his knees, arms and face. Apparently a class-mate – also a refugee – had painted him like a zebra and he had not been able to protest. However, he took school in his stride, apparently under the impression that it was an institution where one was supposed to sit still and understand nothing. For several weeks he spoke not a word in English and then suddenly began to speak the language quite fluently. He continued to speak German at home and rarely mixed his vocabularies and grammar. I understand that this is characteristic for a bilingual child in his circumstances.

Mass movements of populations have created a world in which bilingualism and multilingualism are increasingly common, but it is only recently that the problems arising from this have been properly investigated. In any case I had been asymetrically bilingual from early childhood, speaking German with my parents and Czech with the servants. I had studied Greek and Latin at grammar school, but I had only had a year's English tuition when I came to England for the first time, and only a few weeks of instruction before I settled down in England. My grandchildren suggest irreverently that I have never mastered the language.

Two further observations may be of interest. Struggling with English, I found that I had lost most of my ability to speak Czech. I had also forgotten my French and my Italian, but not German, my mother-tongue. Also 'suppressed' was a vast store of memos and bibliographical data relevant to my previous scientific work. It was several years before I could recall this information at will.

Then there is the problem of translating. I do not normally translate from German into English and vice versa. I operate in either language and often cannot remember which I am using. But there are preferences. Some thoughts – especially those relating to statistics and genetics – come to me in English; others – notably those relating to physiology, medicine and philosophy – naturally in German. Fish taxonomy, which I learned in Roscoff, remains a French subject.

As the summer advanced and German propaganda against Poland intensified, war became more probable. On 17 June, the eve of my father's seventieth birthday, I telephoned him and spoke for the very last time to both my parents.

In Hampstead Garden Suburb gas masks were distributed, the territorials called up, and a week before war was declared, a lorry arrived at our door, bearing parts of a garden shelter. We were the poorest family in the road, and consequently we had not had to order and pay for our 'Anderson' shelter in the usual way, but were given one by the government. In the event we were the only house in our road to have one. A Viennese girl cousin had meanwhile joined our household and helped us dig a hole in the garden for the contraption – a huge box of corrugated iron with two bunks, one above the other. When the first air-raid siren sounded – a false alarm, as it turned out – we had just finished covering the smooth roof with earth and went right in.

For a while during what has become known as 'the phoney war' only the papers and the radio made us aware that hostilities had started. Everything was quiet in our street. The children had two parties in the Anderson. But at College a complex evacuation was mounted. The principal had ordered that all animals in the Zoology Department must be killed. Dozens of large tortoises were rotting on the roof and tropical fish were thrown away as aquaria were emptied. Haldane's geneticists disobeyed the instructions to kill their pure lines of mice and Drosophila, which it had taken years to build up. Like R.A. Fisher and his staff they refused to disperse to Wales or other remote locations. Haldane nailed a poster with the inscription: 'Freedom is in peril – Defend it with all your might' to his door, and sensationally reported confrontations between professors and administrators ensued. A notable rumour had it that Fisher had been involved in a tussle with a college beadle who had tried to prevent the great man from climbing over the spiked railings in Gower Street and had debagged him.

Late in the summer of 1940 the nightly air attacks on London grew in intensity. Even Hampstead Garden Suburb was not immune and we often spent our nights with neighbours' children in the Anderson shelter under our lawn. During the day my work was frequently interrupted by the air-raid sirens and the racket of anti-aircraft guns. My colleagues and I would take our microscopes and our Drosophila cultures to the basement. One terrible night a large part of the College went up in flames, including the library. It was ironic that most of the books of the German department were destroyed by German bombs.

I was suffering at the time a recurrence of my debilitating eye-trouble, one of my eyes being encased in bandages, and I was an out-patient at Moorfields Eye Hospital. When the bombs began to fall in the vicinity of University College, Professor Watson evacuated his department to Aberystwyth, where there was very little space for all of us. So I stayed in London, attended the hospital, and hunted around for another working place.

One day while lunching in the University College cafeteria I found myself sharing a table with Professor J.B.S. Haldane and Helen Spurway. He asked me what I was doing and I told him of my predicament, whereupon he at once offered me a place in his department. It could not have come at a more fortuitous time, and, though we were to have our disagreements, I felt grateful to him ever afterwards.

The bombing intensified and, although the laboratories escaped damage, electricity, water, gas, telephone and heating had been disconnected since the beginning of the war, and Haldane finally gave in and we all looked around for a new home for the department.

5

Working With Haldane

Haldane had a house on the river near Cambridge large enough to accommodate those of his staff who were not engaged in war work, and conveniently adjacent to a cluster of outhouses which Professor Martin, a colleague of Haldane's father, had converted into a laboratory. It seemed ideal for our small group. We went there, enjoyed tea on the lawn, distributed bedrooms and working premises only to learn the next morning that there were insuperable problems over the lease. We returned to our freezing London laboratories which were subject to increasingly frequent bombing raids, and looked around in vain for alternatives.

Help came from an unexpected quarter, R.A. Fisher. Having previously worked at the Rothamsted Experimental Station in the small Hertfordshire town of Harpenden, Fisher had taken his University College team to his old stamping ground, and, on hearing of our plight, he advised Haldane to try to do the same. Negotiations were successful, and we were granted laboratory space in Harpenden 'for the duration'.

Thus it was that Helen Spurway, a colleague who was to become Haldane's second wife, Elizabeth Jermyn, his secretary, Nussy and I climbed into Haldane's small car with the registration letters EGO, and set out one October morning to find a house to live in. Since houses and flats in the country were at a premium as a result of the Blitz, we intended to find a house to share with several of our colleagues, Jimmy Rendel and his wife and Dr Ursula Philip, as well as those named above, as a departmental household. It was not long before we settled on 'Crossways', a Victorian house near the centre of town and only 10 minutes walk from the research station. It was fully furnished, and Nussy and I arranged to loan our London furniture to refugee friends, while bringing to Crossways only the grand piano, some pictures of Prague and a few indispensable books. Whenever I played the piano, which was not frequently, it caused considerable annoyance to the unmusical Haldane. He had brought just one suitcase and a crate of books with him. He set out the collected works of Marx, Lenin and other Socialist writers on a long shelf in the sitting-room, but I never saw anybody reading them.

The house, which has long since been demolished, stood in a mature garden amid large trees, lawns, flower beds and an orchard. There was also a somewhat derelict tennis court. The services of a gardener were included in our contract. He was half-blind.

As a social and socialist experiment our living arrangements left something to be desired. Haldane was the householder and paid the rent. Nussy alternated with Rendel's wife as housekeeper, but Mrs Rendel had a small baby and was more interested in Virginia Woolf, poetry and ghosts than in housekeeping, so very soon it was Nussy who was landed with the shopping and cooking the main meals. Other members of the department undertook the breakfasts, the cleaning, the heating, and various weekend duties. We tried employing servants, but they never stayed. Some stole our rations, others were antagonised by Helen, scared by Haldane, or both.

The interior of the house was murky, the furniture dark and uncouth. When you entered from the beautiful garden it appeared a gloomy, spooky place with long ill-lit corridors and creaking staircases. Nussy and I slept in the main bedroom, the Rendels in the second largest bedroom, our boys in a sizeable laundry cupboard – the only warm room in the house – while Haldane and the others had single rooms. Expenses were shared on a strict points system. As Nussy did most of the housework, our two boys paid half the going rate.

One day George, then five, announced at breakfast that he had counted up the beds in the house and the inhabitants of the house and that there was one bed too few. The announcement was greeted with amusement rather than embarrassment. Haldane was impressed with the sophisticated numeracy of such a small boy. However, the great man was in the process of divorcing his first wife and was most anxious that the 'King's proctor', an official whose duty was to sniff out adultery, should not get wind of his affair with Helen Spurway. So he insisted that we all swear secrecy, threatening that if we did not he would have to dissolve the department. Coming from 'Prof', our nickname for Haldane, a large and rather menacing figure, it should have been an impressive threat, but I have to record that we did not take it too seriously and even adopted it as a slogan, reciting it in unison whenever an occasion arose. Haldane never did dissolve the department, but resigned from the headship many years later.

Helen had become interested in the inheritance of colour and pattern in newts and had brought five crested newts to the house in an aquarium; two males named Fafner and Fasolt, after the giants in Wagner's *Ring*, and three females named after the Rhinemaidens. The aquarium stood in the bay window of the sitting-room and once a week the newts were fed with waterfleas (*Daphnia*). One morning the water in the aquarium appeared slightly discoloured – mostly green but pink where a ray of the sun penetrated – and Haldane and I agreed that the phenomenon was due to the growth of a particular species of unicellular algae, producing what is known as *flos aquae*, the bloom of the water. Haldane pointed this out to all present, including the boys, and we left it at that. The next morning the fluorescence was more marked and in the afternoon one of the female newts, Wellgunde, was found dead, floating on her back; the following morning the other newts were also dead. Discovered next to the aquarium was a bottle of red ink and a dropper. Helen had hysterics, George was identified as the culprit, but Haldane, siding with the boy, opined that this first foray into experimental biology was quite creditable for one of his tender years. I was inevitably reminded of my own juvenile experiments, often much more dangerous than George's.

Between the huge Haldane and my tiny son a strangely touching relationship had grown up. The Prof was very fond of George, but had clearly not the slightest idea how to handle children; consequently George became cheeky. Once when J.B.S. complained about the porridge, mumbling that it was miserably thin gruel, George told him that he was silly to complain; had he not himself brought the oatmeal specially from Scotland? Nussy assumed that Haldane would 'eat George' and fled. But the Prof merely said meekly: 'Quite right, George', and left, grinning and puffing away at his pipe. He reacted quite differently when years later I told him off in similar fashion. My elder son, Peter, less of an extrovert and by no means as aggressive as his brother, never aroused Haldane's interest. Like a pachyderm the Prof had to be pricked or hit hard to take notice.

Haldane was very fond of children in general and sad not to have any of his own. But his manner towards them was incongruous. He could write a charming children's book, *My Friend, Mr Leaky*, but his standard approach to a child was to place himself in all his bulk in front of it and bellow some incomprehensible sentences with all the gentleness of a sergeant-major. This was meant to be funny, but most children were startled by such behaviour and I saw at least one flee in terror. He could be extremely jealous of small children. When visited by photographers and journalists from *Time Magazine*, who had come to write about him, he was peeved to find the children of the household snapped and made a fuss of. In the event *Time* published nothing about him after all.

At the time of the German-Russian pact Haldane thought – perhaps hoped – that he might be arrested as a result of his Soviet sympathies. Accompanying me home from Rothamsted one evening, he told me that he was making arrangements for all his money to be distributed among us, his staff, so that, if he was apprehended, it would not be blocked or confiscated. We all expected the police to come and indeed, one evening when we were sitting at dinner, a policeman did knock at the door. However, he had only called to pass on the complaint of a neighbour, whose dog had allegedly been bitten by Tommy, Helen's fox terrier. Martyrdom did not come Haldane's way.

Nussy and I were in an anomalous situation *vis-à-vis* the authorities. As aliens, albeit friendly ones, we were required to obey a nine o'clock curfew, although our sons, being minors, were under no such constraints.

Nussy had developed the habit of spending one night a week in London. Air raids or not, it was her escape from communal living. One day she was warned that the police had taken to searching the trains for people who were not authorised to travel. So she went to the police station to ask for a permit. What, the police constable wanted to know, was she doing in London?

'Visiting a friend,' said Nussy.

'A boyfriend or a fiancé?' asked the constable, and when Nussy explained that she visited a girlfriend he scratched his head and concluded that that was not sufficient reason for a permit. A male friend would do, but not a female friend. Encouraged by his grin, Nussy asked what would happen to her if she travelled without a permit. He replied: 'Just don't let me catch you!'

The weekly excursions continued.

I was contravening the curfew even more absurdly. I was not permitted to leave the house after nine o'clock but I had also been detailed to do firewatch duty every 10 days at the Experimental Station.

Only twice during the whole war was Harpenden attacked by bombers and the firewatchers at Rothamsted had only one night raid to deal with. That was the night of our arrival, and we had been particularly looking forward to getting some sleep after our exhausting nights in the Hampstead shelter. Mr Bamji, a Parsee colleague, was one of the watchers when a small fire-bomb landed on the flat roof of the entomology building; helped by an Irishman he put it out with the aid of a sand-bucket. Thereafter we used to rag Mr Bamji a good deal because he had not, as required by his creed, worshipped the fire but smothered it.

Often my firewatching companion was Miss Lettice M. Crump, a well-known soil protozoologist. One night we were talking about how biology was changing and Lettice remarked that 'nobody can understand genetics'. I demurred and she challenged me to do something about it. From this casual conversation came my most successful venture in popularising genetics. Without consulting a book I dictated what I thought people should know about the subject, while Lettice wrote it all down and corrected my grammar. Thus many weary hours of firewatching became pleasantly productive, and the book which resulted was published by Penguin after the war.

There is little doubt that the sales of the book were boosted by the Lysenko affair. Twice this century the science of genetics has been muddied by politics. An exaggerated estimate of the role of heredity in the social and cultural sphere culminated in Nazism, the most powerful evil of my lifetime and the most maleficent influence upon it. The role of the majority of German biologists in supporting the

Nazi ideology resulted in an almost total eclipse of genetic research in Germany, lasting at least a generation.

The second blow to genetics originated in the Soviet Union and may be perceived as a reaction to what had taken place in Germany. For the Russians their victory over Germany also implied a victory of the environmentalists over the hereditarians. Hostility towards genetics was nothing new amongst Marxists. In the early years of the last war the Moscow Institute for Human Genetics was disbanded and its director disappeared without trace. The study of human genetics was taboo. Years later when I asked Russian colleagues how they had instructed their students to understand the transmission through generations of blood groups, they just shrugged their shoulders.

Working in England these developments only affected me in the sense that at international conferences I had to listen to lies and deceptions, but for many Eastern bloc biologists the consequences were grave and even, in a few cases, lethal.

But the most destructive influence on genetics in the post-war era relates to the sinister figure of Trophim Denisovich Lysenko. An agricultural student, Lysenko's early work was concerned with seed management and the photo-periodicity of plants. He was credited with the suggestion that seed potatoes could be cut into two or more pieces, each piece containing one eye, instead of planting whole potatoes. This improvement, not, I believe, original to Lysenko, seems to have impressed Stalin, who declared, when Lysenko was being attacked for his Lamarckian* 'transformation experiments' by other Soviet geneticists, that the potato man was right, whereupon genetic research was instantly halted. At some time during these events the eminent plant geneticist, Vavilov, disappeared in mysterious circumstances and his world-famous collection of geographical strains of cultivated plants was dissolved.

The sad Lysenko story illustrates some general and fundamental problems beyond the baleful interference by politicians into scientific research. In the West the results of the Lysenkoists were considered by experimental scientists, who were usually unable to repeat them. But in Russia the problems were also extensively discussed by the philosophers of the Academy, who by some sophistry rejected Mendelian genetics as incompatible with dialect-

*Lamarck was the prophet of the inheritance of acquired characteristics.

ical materialism. To a Western empiricist this may appear irrelevant but to my mind it demonstrates that ideology of whatever kind can have a decisive effect on the questions a scientist attacks. But it is also interesting to try to understand the internal consistency of some of Lysenko's arguments. Denying the existence of genes implies a denial of genetic purity and thus the necessity of using pure lines for genetic experimentation. Crosses between 'impure' stocks can naturally result in any number of recessive mutants. If the appearance of these phenotypes can plausibly be explained by some previous treatment, the case for the inheritance of acquired characteristics seems to be irrefutable – if logic counts for anything within this closed system.

In Britain the reaction to Lysenko and his teachings was interesting. Four eminent geneticists broadcast over four weeks. Three of these broadcasts were concerned with the personality of Lysenko and the politico-scientific situation in the Soviet Union, and dealt with his supposed results from the point of view of orthodox Mendelism. But Haldane tried to persuade his huge audience to keep an open mind and to consider the possibility that Lysenko's claims were justified. Since Haldane was one of the most eminent Mendelians of the century, his broadcast carried considerable weight. Those hostile to Haldane felt that as a Communist he was bound to defend the scientific party line, while a more charitable view was that he genuinely believed in the possibility of some Lamarckian mechanism. Apparently Haldane was aware of the inconsistency between his political creed and his pursuit of scientific truth; he was reported as saying that he would ultimately judge the Soviet regime by its acceptance or refusal of scientific evidence. In the event, for many years now Lysenkoism has been abandoned in Russia and Mendelism is guiding the work of their geneticists.

My own reaction to Haldane's broadcast was a mixture of disgust and admiration. It was clear enough that his arguments were feeble in the extreme and his defence of Lysenko spurious. But I can see how repugnant it must have been to him to provide ammunition for his political adversaries by openly opposing Lysenko and Stalin. Myself I would lack the skill to play devil's advocate in a cause to which I could not subscribe.

Criticism of my book, *Genetics*, was mixed; some friends refused to review it, claiming to be unable to be objective without hurting me; but encouraged by the Lysenko controversy a first and then a second reprint sold very well. *Genetics* has been revised and translated into several languages – into German by Nussy – and still sells after 40 years and despite the immense advances made recently in this field. I put its success down to its non-specialist approach. At the time of writing it, I was in the process of learning genetics myself, and I was thus well qualified to point out the difficulties. Hundreds of books on genetics have been published since, but they either suffer from a subjective and biased viewpoint or they are too technical to be palatable.

I have tried to remember how it was that I first became interested in genetics. As a child I was made aware that certain bodily and behavioural traits 'ran in the family'. My sister 'took after her mother'; I had 'Uncle John's nose'. Heredity seemed to be the occurrence of certain similarities within a family, a matter for wonderment and interest, little more. Years later I found amongst my father's books the 1911 reprint of Mendel's *Pisum* paper; obviously he knew much more about these matters than he had let on. In his forensic work he had become interested in blood groups, but he never discussed these things with me.

I do not recall having been taught any genetics at school. During my biological and medical courses at the German University of Prague, however, I was exposed to a number of short, almost identical and deficient lectures in Mendelism – in zoology, physiology, pathology, forensic medicine etc. – but an extra-curricular genetics course by the plant physiologist, Felix Mainx, aroused my enthusiasm. His demonstrations were convincing, his exposition brilliant. His novel techniques of counting in biology, his propositional calculus, the inventive nature of which I only fully appreciated some time later, fascinated me. Mainx also showed us slides of chromosomes and explained their role in heredity and sex determination; he demonstrated the inheritance of a sex-linked recessive gene giving the example of the white mutant in the fruit-fly *Drosophila Melanogaster*. This gene causes the pigments in the eyes of the flies, which are normally red, not to form, so that a white eye develops. Females from a pure-bred white line mated to males from a pure-bred red-eyed line ('wild type') produce only white-eyed sons and red-eyed daughters. I had some ideas concerning the effects of the loss of eye pigment on the visual performance of the flies, which in fact I was to test many years later, and so I asked Mainx to let me have some flies from his pure stocks and to teach me the techniques of handling and breeding *Drosophila*.

Before embarking on my own experiments, however, I wanted to repeat his, but the results were not at all as I had expected. All the offspring of my crosses, whether male or female, had red eyes! And I had taken great pains to ensure the virginity of the females.

I was too inexperienced to realise that startling results, especially in a field new to the research worker, are usually the consequence of some silly mistake. Fortunately, before stunning Mainx with my 'fundamental discovery', I discovered my mistake. Not knowing much about insect morphology I had confused males and females. I had mistaken the ovipositor of the female for a penis, and the rounded abdomen of the male for a female characteristic. When I tried again and set up the correct matings I got the anticipated results. The only consequence of my blunder was to hone my critical faculties, when conducting experiments.

With the success of *Genetics* I enjoyed a taste of what it must be like to be a celebrity. It was satisfactory to watch in Foyle's one's book selling like hot cakes, to be recognised in Bellagio after the publication of the Italian edition, to find copies on an Israeli kibbutz or a rubber plantation in Amazonia, and to be told by one's incredulous children that they had 'actually seen somebody read a copy in a bus'. Paul Jennings poked gentle fun at the book in the *News Chronicle*, but most gratifying of all were the remarks of some quite celebrated junior colleagues who told me that my little book had got them interested in genetics. It was widely used, though never intended, as a textbook in grammar schools. A nonagenarian, an alumnus of the Galton Laboratory, told me that he had travelled to town and climbed two flights of stairs just to thank me for writing it.

But the popularity of a scientist cannot compare, I am glad to say, with that of footballers or actors. As proof I can attest that I have been far more frequently mistaken for Burt Lancaster, whom I must somehow resemble, than recognised for myself.

The evenings at Crossways were sometimes quite diverting. Haldane took it upon himself to read us the whole of Byron's *Don Juan* and *Childe Harold*, as well as some Scottish ballads. Rendel was an accomplished bridge player, tried to teach us to play, and regularly beat Haldane, who did not like it. Music he abhorred, and

my playing the piano and singing must have caused him considerable pain. The boys played halma and worked at jigsaw puzzles. We
read. We switched the radio on for the news.

Other members of the department visited us. Hans Gruneberg,
who worked on hereditary disorders in mice, came, and Cyril
Gordon, an ebullient South African, doing operational research at
the War Office. There were other visitors.

One afternoon I went into the garden for some vegetables and
was surprised to see over a hedge Haldane walking with a middle-
aged man, upon whose head was a contraption which looked like an
inverted lavatory. A top secret development, this was an early
model of the 'snorkel', and the man had been sent by the Admiralty
to discuss its potential for rescuing sailors from drowning.

Haldane had been interested in the physiology of respiration
since he was a boy. His father had invented an apparatus for
measuring the uptake of oxygen by the blood and was a leading
authority on gas exchange in the lungs. He had taken his son down
the mines at a time when canaries were still being used to test the
presence of carbon monoxide in the air. Haldane himself had been
commissioned by the trade unions before the war to investigate the
death of the crew of the submarine *Thetis*. Partly as a result of his
report on this tragedy, he was asked to lead a civilian team
investigating submarine escapes.

I, too, had been interested in respiration, albeit at a cellular level,
and had published a paper on the measurement of oxygen uptake
of single-cell organisms. Consequently I was delighted to join
Haldane's group. It seemed to me a better contribution to the war
effort than joining the British or Czech armies – the Czech army had
too many doctors anyway. Exposing myself to mixed atmospheres
at high pressures and to the hazards of decompression was both
more dangerous and more interesting than hospital service. It
meant that I did not have to submit to military discipline and could
continue my ordinary research, because it was not safe to conduct
our experiments too frequently. Most important of all, I could spend
much of my time with my family.

Haldane's civilian group was a mixed bunch, comprising
members of the department, old research associates, and political
refugees. The most eminent was Dr Negrin, President in Exile of the
Spanish Republic, and also a physiologist. We worked parallel with

a naval team, which did the 'wet' experiments, using diving gear and water tanks, while we worked with respirators and in compression cylinders. Our brief was to replicate the conditions which might arise in a damaged submarine, and to discover an ideal gas mixture for the respirators to facilitate the escape of those trapped underwater.

The sudden decompression of a diver causes 'bends', severe pains caused by nitrogen bubbles in small blood vessels. Under high pressure an excess of nitrogen dissolves in the blood, and this is released when the pressure is suddenly eased. One of our tasks was to take measurements for a decompression table, which would relate the severity and duration of pressure to safe decompression procedures. 'Bends' can be avoided if nitrogen is removed from what the victim breathes while under pressure; either he should breathe pure oxygen or a mixture of oxygen and the inert gas, helium.

The air in a submerged and damaged submarine deteriorates in several ways, for instance through the escape of acid fumes from batteries or from engines, and, as long as any of the crew survive, these exhale carbon dioxide, which cannot always be efficiently removed. In our experiments we exposed each other to gas mixtures rich in CO_2 and at pressures from 1 to 10 atmospheres approximately corresponding to depths from zero to 90 metres.

We needed four participants for these experiments, the subject and an inside observer within the cylinder, an outside observer who could watch the two through a porthole and speak to them by telephone, and an engineer (usually a naval rating) to manipulate the flow of gases and watch the pressure gauges. Having entered the cylinder one banged a spanner at the wall and was answered with three bangs from without. Then compressed air flowed in through a valve, filling the cylinder with a loud hiss. It became noticeably warmer and one's ear-drums began to ache from the pressure, which could be eased by swallowing hard or holding one's nose and blowing it. When the required pressure was reached one noticed that the voice of one's companion seemed to be coming from a long way away and the air became 'thick'. When flapping a piece of paper, one was aware of considerably more resistance than under normal conditions.

The next step was for one of those inside the compression chamber to don a respirator delivering the particular gas mixture that was being tested, and to undertake various tasks and observations. One's mental arithmetic might be tested, or some simple mechanical skills, such as putting metal balls into holes or joining and separating nuts and bolts. The inside observer would watch the behaviour and general condition of the subject, and, if everything went well, telephone when the experiments were finished and bang on the wall for decompression. As the air escaped with a hiss, the temperature dropped and the cylinder filled with fog. Again the pain in the ears had to be relieved as before. Decompression had to be effected in stages, and could last for several hours. There were crises. Sometimes there were air-raid warnings and on one occasion bombs fell in the vicinity and decompression was hastily effected.

From our small sample I was interested to observe that civilian scientists and naval ratings reacted rather differently to the stresses of our experimentation. As long as things remained tolerable, the sailors were more disciplined and complained less, but when conditions became critical or got out of control, the scientists, and notably the women amongst the scientists, were less inclined to panic, probably because they undertood better the nature of the research.

The most dramatic incidents occurred in the experiments with oxygen under high (partial) pressures. Once when Haldane, as subject, and I, as inside observer, were inside the cylinder, I noticed that, while he was doing his sums, his face had begun to twitch, a sign that general convulsions and loss of consciousness are imminent. At once I pulled the mouthpiece of the respirator, through which he breathed oxygen, out of Haldane's mouth. Instead of displaying gratitude he became annoyed and confused, accusing me of ruining the experiment and bellowing that I should 'get out'. By the time I had explained to him that it would have needed several elephants to have opened the outlet in the compression chamber, he had recovered sufficiently to see the funny side of the episode.

On another occasion Helen Spurway was the experimental subject and I was again the inside observer. Without any apparent warning Helen fell down and started to convulse. When I removed the mouthpiece, I found that she had dislodged her lower jaw, a condition which can lead to swallowing the tongue and possibly death by choking. I took the jaw in both hands and relocated it. I then banged on the wall and telephoned to demand immediate decompression. Haldane and a young naval surgeon tried to look into the cylinder but the fog and condensation on the window made it impossible. Meanwhile Helen had had several more convulsions, and I had had to put the jaw back several times. Everybody was relieved when, an hour later, we were released.

Although I never myself had an oxygen convulsion I did lose consciousness on several occasions when exposed to high concentrations of carbon dioxide in the air. It was not pleasant. Initially I had the feeling of choking and tried to breathe more deeply, which only made things worse. A severe headache would follow, and this would gradually dissolve into unconsciousness. On one such occasion a record exists of my last words before I was disconnected from the respirator, and these display the conflicts a scientist experiences in self-experiments. At first I complained, shouting that it was 'too much', but then I added 'perhaps not!' and passed out. After regaining consciousness a period of confusion inevitably followed. One sailor and Miss Jermyn, whom we had all believed to be an atheist, asked whether they were in heaven. I thought that it was morning and that I was in bed.

We heard a rumour that one of the sailors in the parallel group had died doing an escape exercise. We had no fatalities but Jimmy Rendel developed spontaneous pneumothorax, which meant that one or other of his lungs was liable to collapse without any apparent trigger. The collapse of one lung is alarming, and if both lungs collapse then one dies rather quickly. To prevent this I built an aspirator from two huge laboratory bottles and some rubber tubing. This contraption, which would have enabled me to reflate the collapsed lungs, was kept in a cupboard in my room at Crossways, but was never used.

The prolonged periods of decompression were ideal for reading. During one of them I was reading in *Nature* an article by the Astronomer Royal which rather annoyed me. It was 1943 and the 400th anniversary of the death of Copernicus was being celebrated with the Polish government in London making great play of the fact that Copernicus was a Pole. While it was a reasonable claim, if nationality in the modern sense can be applied to anybody born in the fifteenth century, what was not tenable was the assertion that the Polishness of Copernicus could also be deduced from his mother's maiden name, Watzenrode, which is of course an obvious German name. My annoyance at this cavalier kind of scholarship had been aroused by previous similar claims by London exiles designed to deny greatness to any German. Beethoven had been claimed as Dutch, Kepler as Czech, Schweitzer as French, and so on.

When I told Haldane who was sitting next to me in the cylinder that I would write a letter of protest to *Nature*, he just looked at me through his huge glasses and said nothing. The editors replied politely that perhaps in the circumstances it might be inadvisable to publish my letter, but shortly afterwards a leader appeared, pointing out that scientific honesty was impugned by spurious politically motivated claims and quoted the examples I had sent them, amongst others. I felt gratified to live and work in England, where, in the middle of a ferocious war, I was able both to help in the fight against the Nazis and to repudiate jingoistic propaganda.

But the high pressure experiments were only a part of our team's war effort. We were also required to undertake some mathematical work for the army. I spent hours sitting at an electromechanical calculator and 'solving' some intricate differential equations by iteration, that is to say repeating the same procedures with improved numbers. I had no idea what these equations represented, nor whether our results were ever used. With modern computers the calculations, which took me weeks, could have been completed in minutes, if not seconds.

Meanwhile I was continuing with my research at the Rothamsted Experimental Station. Founded in 1834 by Sir John Bennett Lawes, it had grown into the foremost institute of its kind in the British Empire, possibly in the world. Here, specific research in soil composition and experimental fertilisers was carried on as well as study into the general theory of planning and analysing quantitative experiments. Exposure to this kind of applied work was new to me and had a profound effect; watching my colleagues at Rothamsted persuaded me that research directed towards a practical goal could be much more difficult than some kinds of free-ranging 'basic' research.

One result of these contacts with planned applied work was a short paper: 'A factorial experiment on the mineral requirements of *Drosophila*.'* The American geneticist and statistician, R. Pearl, and some of his pupils had spent considerable time trying to determine the mineral requirements in a feeding substrate for the fruit-fly, at

American Naturalist, 77, 1943, 376–80.

that time the most important organism in genetical research. But when I used their published formula, many fewer flies emerged than from the usual maize-molasses medium. So I set up a 'factorial' experiment, as proposed by R.A. Fisher, applying each of Pearl's five inorganic ingredients, singly, in combinations, and in varying quantities. Including repetitions, 96 cultures were set up. The result was unequivocal. One of Pearl's constituents, Rochelle salt, was harmful, another – calcium chloride – superfluous and the others required slightly different concentrations; and this result was achieved in one go lasting barely three weeks, no more than 20 working hours in total. Pearl's group had laboured for at least a year. I saw my medium being used in several laboratories and the experiment given as an example in a textbook of statistics.

Overall Rothamsted influenced my work enormously. Where I had been accustomed to depend on the intuitive planning of experiments and on the uncertain validation of results, now I had acquired a more reliable quantitative approach. Additionally research in some of the biological departments had a more specific effect. These were the departments concerned with entomology, including the bee sub-department, insecticides and plant pathology. C.B. Williams, the head of entomology, and an expert on insects and their biology, was particularly interested in migration and flight. After a conversation with him I started research on the correlation between sensory equipment and flight apparatus in insects, in particular whether the possession and perfection of ocelli – the small eyes on the back of insects' heads – went together with the possession and size of wings. The results were positive and intriguing. Beetles excepted, all winged orders, families and species of insects also have ocelli, and those without wings lack them. The same holds true within each species.

Finally I found within the literature a drawing of a mosaic ant, one side of which was worker-shaped, the other side queen-shaped. On the worker side no trace of wings was found and only one-and-a-half small ocelli, while on the queen side wings had developed and one-and-a-half larger ocelli occurred. Clearly the development of wings and ocelli is governed in all these instances by a common factor, but what is it?

It is unlikely ever to be a single gene. A number of mutants in

Drosophila produce wingless flies, while others deprive them of ocelli; but the wingless flies have perfect ocelli, and the flies lacking ocelli have perfect wings.

Could it be that the development of both wings and ocelli is controlled by a hormone, possibly the 'juvenile' hormone? This seems to be the case in insects like grasshoppers, bugs and others, which, unlike moths, butterflies or bees, do not pupate but pass through a number of nymphal stages before they reach adulthood. In those species wings and ocelli grow and differentiate in parallel. But it is difficult to see how a hormone could affect one side of the ant mosaic mentioned above but not the other. The nature of the common factor remains unknown, but I suspect that its identification will play an important role in future ontogenetic research and evolutionary speculation.

Interactions with my colleagues at Rothamsted were social as well as scientific. I was even made a member of the Staff Club, joined the Music Society, and even played hockey, both for the station team and for a St Albans club. I acquired lifelong friends.

Red Gables, once the home and studio of the painter Salisbury, was our Rothamsted Clubhouse. Here my London colleagues and I made the acquaintance of our hosts 'for the duration of the war'. Most were friendly towards us, but not all. The head of botany, a fierce, elderly lady, who was jealous of her accumulated stores of chemicals and equipment, burst into our laboratory on our second day at Rothamsted and accused me of ordering numerous items to which I had no claim. The truth was that she had confused me with the newly appointed head of the biochemistry department, who had also arrived the previous day and was fully within his rights to order whatever he needed. But she became so aggressive that I could not resist telling her that, though innocent on this occasion, I would certainly demand chemicals from the stores just as soon as I needed them. This led to a stormy meeting between Haldane and Sir John Russell, the station director, as a result of which Haldane had to bring from London any chemicals that I needed for my experiments, despite the large quantities kept in store at Rothamsted.

More bizarre were the reactions of another of my new colleagues, an entomologist, who developed a complex of paranoid fantasies about me, of which I only gradually became aware. I believe that the main reason for his resentment – he accused me of coveting his job –

was that, having been too young to serve in the First World War, he was not permitted to serve in the second either, being in a 'reserved occupation'. This product of a famous public school and an Oxford college was reduced to the ranks of the Home Guard, and thrown into the company of a German-speaking, suspect, and possibly treacherous character like myself. Some time later he came to my desk one morning and announced that he was glad that the danger of invasion had receded, because that relieved him of his duty to hand me over to the police if fighting were to break out on British soil. When I pointed out to him that the French police had handed people like me straight to the SS and certain death, and that something similar might happen to me here, he added that he would nevertheless have had me arrested because that was international law. I thanked him for this information and added that I now knew whom to kill quickly in the event of the Germans invading England after all. The following day he brought me as a token of good will three eggs freshly laid by his own hens. A precious gift indeed and we ate them with considerable relief and amusement.

Dr Frederic Tattersfield was the head of the insecticide department, a chemist of the old school, with a friendly disposition. One fine afternoon we were having tea on the lawn when we discovered that we had a common interest in the same experimental creature, a strain of *Drosophila*, which, unlike other flies of the same species and most other insects, is killed by a few seconds of exposure to carbon dioxide and low temperatures. This curious susceptibility is inherited in a non-Mendelian fashion through the female and only rarely and impermanently through the male. (It has since been established that the CO_2 susceptibility is conferred by a virus in the way of an infection.) Shortly after two French biologists, L'Heretier and Teissier, had discovered this strain, France had fallen and their stock of susceptibles was unobtainable in Britain. I had no idea that Dr Tattersfield had already acquired a culture, and I had collected another from Herman Muller, later to be a Nobel Laureate, through Haldane employing the good offices of the USAF – and, allegedly, a parachutist. Tattersfield's interest lay in the exceptional toxicity of CO_2 as an insecticide, while I was more concerned with the mode of transmission and the properties of the agent.

With young Avrion Mitchison (now Professor Mitchison) helping me, we transplanted larval ovaries from my susceptible strain into resistant normal larvae, where they attached themselves to the oviducts, with the result that the emerging female flies produced eggs not only from their own ovaries but also from the implants. When exposed to CO_2 in the cold, only the 'legitimate' offspring were killed; the descendants of the implants survived. Reciprocal experiments led to the same conclusion, and I concluded that the agent for the susceptibility could not be transferred by transplantation and that the agent was not a virus. (Later experiments by others cast doubts on the validity of these conclusions.)

The original CO_2 susceptible stock was unique. The French found no other susceptible flies in their laboratory stocks; nor did anyone else. I was intrigued that some *Drosophila* flies trapped outside Rothamsted were killed by exposure to CO_2, and I naturally assumed that I might have caught offspring of escaped or discarded flies from Dr Tattersfield's experiments. But I came across the same phenomena further afield. There seemed to be susceptibles all over the place. Testing *D. Melanogaster* stocks, which had not been stored in laboratories for too long, I found that samples from both the new world and the old contained varying percentages of susceptibles, from 0 to 100 per cent. This poses an interesting epidemiological problem: in the laboratory all susceptible females are found to transmit susceptibility to 100 per cent of their offspring; but when you deal with populations containing both susceptible and resistant flies, the latter soon disappear. How then did it happen that susceptibility seemed to have vanished in all but one of the established laboratory stocks? And why are not all wild populations 100 per cent susceptible?

While my war work and my regular research were continuing satisfactorily, things were not running so smoothly on the domestic scene. After a year and a half of communal living at Crossways centrifugal forces began to exert themselves. Some originals moved out and were replaced by newcomers. So when an opportunity presented itself, Nussy and I bought a small house on what were then the outskirts of Harpenden, and found ourselves living amongst the ordinary people: postmen, technicians, artisans of all kinds. They were a friendly and neighbourly lot. My popularity grew when I delivered our neighbour's baby. The mother was the wife of a policeman.

Our boys grew up and flourished in the local school. Freed from the communal housekeeping, Nussy found a pleasant part-time job in the Rothamsted library. At the beginning of the war a collection of some 200 herbals and old books about plants and agriculture had been hurriedly removed to the basement. Now that the bombardments had subsided, the books were brought back upstairs, only for it to be discovered that several valuable volumes appeared to be missing, while the surviving books were in a chaotic state. The professional librarian was away on active service, and his substitute, an elderly and eccentric Russian princess, terrified the local girls into inefficiency. Nussy's knowledge of European languages was useful, and she was able to put the collection back in order, and to find some of the missing volumes, which more than covered her modest pay.

The war dragged on. Defeats and victories abroad, rationing and the deterioration of living standards at home imperceptibly changed people's attitudes and expectations. Nussy and I were most concerned about the uncertain fate of our families. Rumours of deportations, of concentration camps and gas chambers became more and more horribly credible as the years passed. We received no news of my parents and my sister, nor of Nussy's mother. But we did manage to keep in contact with the combatant members of the families. My brother had managed to join the Czech army in Athens and had fought under British command in Africa and under Russian command in the Carpathians. Occasionally aerograms arrived from him announcing transfers, typhus, woundings and his wedding. Nussy's three brothers, officers in the Yugoslav army, were captured by the Germans after just a few days fighting. Thanks to the Red Cross they were able to keep in contact with us and even received some of our parcels. But from friends at home and other more distant relatives we received no news whatever.

In London exiled governments and *émigré* organisations proliferated as more and more European states succumbed to the Nazis. I joined an association of Czech doctors and scientists – most of them German-speaking Jews – who were making grandiose and utopian plans for 'after the war'.

One day two gentlemen whom I had never met before, nor have seen since, arrived unannounced on my doorstep, introduced themselves – their names were Muller and Schmidt, or something similar – and said that they were the emissaries of the Sudeten-German Committee of Anti-Fascists, and that they represented a non-party organisation which was trying to unite all German-speaking Czechoslovak citizens in the fight against Hitler. What they did *not* say was that they excluded all Social Democrats (these had been organised by Wenzel Jaksch). It became apparent later that they were in fact a Communist front organisation. The two gentlemen were well informed about my scientific work, and complimented me on it and they persuaded me to attend one of their meetings. The following day I read a report of the proceedings in which my short contribution appeared as the very opposite of what I had said. I left the group and never had anything more to do with them.

I gave a couple of lectures on genetics to another small and short-lived group which called itself the Free German University; this too, it transpired, was organised by Communists. These insignificant brushes with Communism made me ineligible in the McCarthy era for an American visa, and I still have difficulty in obtaining one today.

I was taken one evening to an Austrian club in London at which Arthur Koestler read part of his great novel of Communist disillusion, *Sonnenfinsternis*, or *Darkness at Noon*. I was much impressed, but in the ensuing debate I pointed out some slight inaccuracies in his technical details about submarines, and this had the effect of clouding somewhat our relationship which went back many years to the time when Koestler, as science correspondent of the Berlin *Vossiche Zeitung*, reviewed my first book on *Paramecium*. In his student days he had been a contemporary of Nussy's eldest brother at Vienna University and, like me, a guest in their Yugoslav home.

Towards the end of the war, when Germany was being devastated by British and American bombing raids, the thoughts of the allies turned to the general problems of assuring future peace in Europe, and the particular problems of the re-establishment of civilisation in Germany. I wished to participate and wrote a few popular articles on scientific matters which were published in a German-language newspaper and distributed by the British occupying forces; I also broadcast on similar themes, although, because of my 'Austrian' accent, I was not considered a suitable reader.

More rewarding were the lectures which I gave on behalf of the Ministry of Defence to German prisoners of war. The camps which I visited were huge but consisted only of 'other ranks', since the officers had been removed to other places for re-education and rabid Nazis to special smaller camps. But there were medical officers in the camps I visited, and sometimes they were from the German University in Prague.

One night I arrived at Mildenhall, an East Anglian sugar beet town, having been the only passenger on a darkened train. The dimly-lit platform was deserted and somewhere in the distance I could hear gunfire from an anti-aircraft battery. Soon I was aware of an approaching car and was confronted by two men in uniform, who clicked their heels and asked me in German whether I was Dr Kalmus, the expected lecturer. There was no sign of any English guard. Listening to the bursts of shell-fire, which had become more frequent, and looking at the searchlight beams in the cloudy sky, the thought occurred that an encounter with two German soldiers across the sea would have had fatal implications for me.

It turned out that the man who first addressed me was the cultural organiser in the camp, while the other man, the driver, came from the Sudetenland. At the entrance to the camp we were stopped by an armed sentry – also a German – and given a cup of tea. Then I was led to the large mess hall in which I was to deliver my lecture. All this time I had not seen a Briton. They were allegedly with their girlfriends in the local pub. Introduced to some 70 or 80 men I again could not avoid speculating as to my fate were I to be confronted with a similar group of men on the continent. I spoke on the role of plant and animal breeding in post-war reconstruction. My main topics were crop and stock improvement, but I also dealt with related matters, such as the feeding of grain to animals instead of directly to hungry people, of the different speeds at which depleted stocks of poultry, pigs, cattle or horses could be made good, and other topics of practical interest. During the discussion I was asked my views on those racial theories which had been fed to my audience over many years, and had to deal with them in a few minutes. I had no idea what impact I was having on my bewildered, suspicious and resentful audience, but one of my ex-students did at least propose a vote of thanks before I was driven back to the station.

After about 30 or 40 of such lectures I received a letter from the Ministry of Defence objecting to my discussing controversial matters, and requesting me to stick to my subject during the discussions as well as during my lectures. I replied that I could not refuse to answer any questions put to me by the prisoners, and that was the end of the lectures.

There was a prisoner of war camp not far from Harpenden, and shortly after the war, when Nussy was preoccupied with our new daughter, Elsa, we were glad to avail ourselves of the help in the garden of a couple of Germans from the camp. They were forbidden to accept money for this work, and so we took to inviting them into the house and plying them with tea and cigarettes. The two most regular visitors came from areas which had been occupied by the Red Army. They had had no news from home for several years and were extremely worried. I think they enjoyed coming to our house, and one of them sent me Christmas cards for 10 years thereafter.

I remember two incidents involving these men, one poignant, one funny. The first concerned a friend of mine's original meeting with them. He had fought on the allied side and had been wounded, but had not met any enemy soldiers, except in battle. At first he refused to meet them, but when I insisted that there was no war at our tea-table, he eventually agreed to join us. The second concerned a duck. This unfortunate bird had been accidentally killed by one of the prisoners while driving a tractor. The owner of the duck complained and the man had a week's camp money docked, which he greatly resented. He was no better pleased when his friends, Nussy and I, could not help laughing. I enquired whether he had demanded the dead bird which he had paid for, but the idea clearly struck him as absurd.

As soon as the German defeat seemed inevitable, the provost of University College ordered the dispersed departments back to London. The return was as badly timed as our over-hasty evacuation at the start of the war had been, for no sooner had we restarted our experimental work than the V2 bombs began to fall on London. I watched one of them during my lunch-break on the roof of the department. A loud bang, a huge dust-cloud where a block of buildings had been, and seconds later the sinister sound of the supersonic rocket. But not too many of the V2s reached their target, and the College remained in London thereafter, while I, staying on in Harpenden, became a regular commuter, and indeed I still travel to town several times a week.

An autobiography is not the appropriate medium for a detailed analysis of other people, but since J.B.S. Haldane has featured so prominently in this one, it seems not out of place to comment a little on his eccentric personality and erratic behaviour, at least in as much as it impinged upon my own work and career.

He was very good at choosing able collaborators and he gave them the greatest freedom in the pursuit of their researches. For this I am grateful. But he was a poor administrator and clumsy in his personal relationships. Being more intelligent than most, with a privileged background and an intimidating physique, he tried to appear an egalitarian and often got away with it, but he never learned to reconcile his Socialist principles with his own behaviour. I believe that I understood him better than most and, in so far as professor and lecturer, local celebrity and immigrant, can ever be friends, we got on pretty well for many years. There occurred, however, a bizarre episode which neither of us could comfortably handle, and which did me, or at least my career, some damage.

Haldane's detestation of the bourgeoisie was constantly reinforced by Helen Spurway. She had grown up in poverty and had accumulated grudges against middle-class professionals, clergymen, lawyers, and most especially doctors.

One morning Helen's assistant, an unmarried mother of a five-year-old boy, had telephoned in some agitation to report that her child had been sick in the night and that she had called the doctor, who had yet to come. At once Helen inveighed against middle-class doctors who care nothing about working-class children, considering that they might as well die. An hour later the assistant rang again. The doctor had now called, had seen the little boy, had diagnosed the trouble as probably appendicitis, and had promised to call again at noon. In a state of high excitement Helen repeated her accusations and, in the presence of Haldane, asked me to go and see the child 'to arrange things'. I considered her demand unreasonable and said so. The doctor was keeping the child under observation which was perfectly proper in the circumstances. I was not on the medical register and had therefore no authority to get the boy into hospital. I tried in vain to explain all this. There was no further news from the mother, and in the common-room after lunch, Haldane hurled accusations at me, whereupon I called him an ass. There was consternation among the half-dozen or so witnesses when Haldane shouted out that he would ruin me and ran away.

The consequences of this ludicrous episode were manifold, and some were serious. Now I had to tolerate being associated with a

Communist chief and suspected of sharing his opinions, while being personally alienated from him. Yet I owed him considerable gratitude for what he had previously done for me, and did not feel that I should tell anybody about our differences. Meanwhile Helen Spurway told anybody who was prepared to listen that it was quite remarkable that Kalmus could write even tolerable English.

At that time I was responsible for arranging the departmental seminars to which I frequently invited foreign colleagues, who might be visiting Britain, and who could not always attend at the traditional time for the seminar. Before changing the advertised time I would of course telephone my senior colleagues to enquire whether they could manage the new timetable. After our contre-temps Haldane would always refuse to commit himself, and then accuse me of trying to keep him away from the seminars. So I stopped telephoning him or talking to him and only communicated through official letters. He still complained, but never missed a seminar.

There were other manifestations of hostility. Once at a conversazione at the Royal Society, my friend C.R. Ribbands and I were exhibiting some shared research concerning the colony odour of honey-bees. Onlookers were astonished when Haldane, who had had absolutely no hand in this work, planted himself directly in front of us and proceeded to explain the exhibit.

On another occasion he kept me out of a newly funded 'communications centre' at University College despite the fact that I was the only member of his department who had worked and published in this field. A letter to the provost put things right; I was duly co-opted. However, neither of us ever went there and the project collapsed.

We did manage in time to achieve a kind of truce. At public meetings we concealed our animosity and few suspected that there were any problems between us.

He was very gratified when in the course of studying tone-deafness I found him to be blatantly tone-deaf, and he told everyone about this disability and would have liked me to find him colour-blind also. In this I could not oblige him, and the best I could do was to tell him that his eyes were of slightly different colours. We never discussed the visual arts and I did not get the impression that he was particularly interested in them. But he did study cartoons featuring himself with great care.

Official and even private celebrations in his honour he did not easily bear. When a farewell dinner was organised by his colleagues on the eve of his departure for India, he refused to sit in the place of honour, next to his wife, and managed to go the whole evening without a drink, except for a glass of water. Seeing him sitting so abstemiously in his ill-fitting clothes, one did not know whether to laugh or cry.

In many ways he was a battlefield of conflicting ideas. He was exceedingly concerned with scientific truth and even wrote a paper on how to fake scientific material and how to detect such fakes. One of his conclusions was that to fake data convincingly was often more laborious than to do honest, solid work. He was not over-concerned with always being right and often enjoyed pointing out in front of audiences and even students how he had been shown to have been wrong. But where the emotions were concerned it was a different matter. In politics his dislike of the establishment overrode his honesty.

He kept his scientific and political activities as separate as possible, and told me that I would be well advised not to go and listen to him addressing public meetings. He used to say that he owed much of his department to two men: Hitler, who had created so many refugees, and Rockefeller, whose foundation paid them. In fact, of course, Haldane went out of his way to help displaced scholars. He knew very well, I am sure, how deeply in his debt we all were. As a lecturer he seemed to find it far easier to present material of which he had only second-hand knowledge than to talk about his own researches. Some of his addresses on contemporary issues were superb, and his undergraduate lectures excellent. Indeed the best of his articles and talks rank with the finest examples of contemporary prose. But when lecturing to a seminar or a learned society about some special piece of research he could be quite unintelligible and his presentation of the material painful to listen to.

He knew a great deal about the monarchy and the church on the principle that one should know one's adversaries. He published a pedigree of haemophilia in the Royal Family, and he told the Duke of Edinburgh at a congress on genetics that it was unstable for a modern nation to have a sovereign. Generally he refused to have any dealings with the Court. However, I did hear him once during a weekend symposium at Cumberland Lodge proposing the Queen's health, and referring to her as 'our generous host'.

He sometimes agreed to co-operate with the Anglican Church, and submitted to the Convocation evidence on genetics relating to the Impediments to Marriage. He admired the Church's considerable tolerance, the relative independence of incumbents, once they had been appointed, and he thought rather highly of the ideology of a few churchmen. Judaism, Hinduism and Buddhism attracted him. I do not know what he thought about Rome.

Among his idiosyncrasies was an acute aversion to conventional politeness. No woman could offer him tea and ask him how much milk he wanted; he had to put the milk in himself. He always refused to take anyone's chair, even when a young undergraduate invited him to sit down, but he would always gratefully and rather ostentatiously accept the offer of an air cushion or a bolster pointing out that he had damaged his back in some self-experimentation. Once he arrived, as he often did, late for a lecture. All the seats were taken and nobody offered him a chair. He groaned loudly and lay down in a corner on the floor. It was not a lot of good asking him vaguely how he was, but detailed inquiries as to how his organs were functioning would be answered in full, and it was not easy to avoid a clinical investigation.

He expected his bed and food to be ready at any time, and if he was obliged at some particularly unearthly hour to wait to be fed, he would growl: 'All right. I want a glass of cold water and a deck-chair in the coal shed.' Sometimes he got both. Most people thought him a surprisingly formidable and even frightening figure of a man. His great bulk, bald head, and heavy horn-rimmed glasses were partly responsible for this, but so was his uncompromising manner. It was not so much what he said – sometimes he said nothing but brooded in silence – as his intonation. I remember at a bridge party when he disapproved of one of my wife's bids. All he said was: 'I beg your pardon', but Nussy was mortally offended, and the incident in former times would have led to a duel.

He either believed or pretended to believe that businessmen were petty thieves and proletarians paragons of honesty. When our landlord at Harpenden came to look at some things he had left in the attic, Haldane went upstairs as soon as the landlord had left to see 'whether his golden watch was still there'. In the same week a greatly honoured maid who had helped in our communal household stole 25lbs of sugar, almost our entire stock, to make marmalade. Thus were his suspicions increased, and there was a crisis at Crossways. He began to accuse all and sundry of stealing his 'blue socks' or his 'warm pants'. An investigation showed that he had never had any blue socks, but the pants which were in tatters had been used to wipe the floor with, but were now returned to him, washed and ironed.

The testimonials he supplied were most peculiar. Of one pupil – now a most eminent man – he wrote: 'He has not stolen anything and is the holder of a season ticket.' Of another: 'He has published many papers, some of which are in fact right.' His interview technique could be quite distressing. Once he introduced a candidate for a job by saying: 'My colleague here thinks you might be very useful in the department. I don't think that, but we shall see.'

He appeared blunt; in reality he was shy. As a result he used elaborate means of communicating with us. He would leave documents on colleagues' desks 'as if by accident'. And through these calculated leaks we learned quite a bit about his private affairs – a will, a letter to the provost in which he pleaded for those of us who were not yet well established, circulars about savings and investment that had been addressed to him. We never mentioned these circuitous messages, and they vanished as mysteriously as they had appeared. Conversations, too, had to be oblique. We learned to say things like 'friendship between a professor and a younger colleague dependent on him is a difficult proposition' or 'one cannot really be expected to educate one's superiors', than to come directly out with the necessary home truth. Bluntness in others was anathema to him.

At his farewell dinner on the eve of his tragicomic emigration to India, we finally made our peace. The last time I saw him he was in University College Hospital after his operation for an intestinal cancer. To the embarrassment of the ward sister he insisted on showing me his wound. We also discussed one of the rhymes in his famous poem: 'Cancer's a Funny Thing'. This is the one first published in the *New Statesman* which begins:

I wish I had the voice of Homer
To sing of rectal carcinoma,
Which kills a lot more chaps, in fact,
Than were bumped off when Troy was sacked . . .

Colleagues have told me that even on his deathbed he accused them of all sorts of bourgeois hypocrisies.

Death, dying and immortality were subjects about which he felt the greatest ambivalence.* It was a lifelong preoccupation. Deeply affected by his father's death, he also saw a good many men die during the First World War. He was very much afraid of bombs, and at the start of the blitz we spent a great deal of time traipsing downstairs with microscopes, notebooks, and the rest of the paraphernalia. One particularly wild night, when bombs were falling, anti-aircraft guns bellowing and sirens wailing, we spent together in the basement of Sir Julian Huxley's flat. The pets were much disturbed. Haldane crouched in a chair in his usual posture, with a writing-pad on his knees, but he looked peculiar. When I took his pulse, it was hard, small and very irregular. I was more frightened by this than by the whole bombardment.

In contrast to his egotistical attitude to death was his experimental and often light-hearted attitude to the process of dying, which I observed during the submarine experiments. On the evening before his cancer operation in London, he wrote out two telegrams addressed to his wife in India. One read: 'Haldane died from cancer operation. Please send directives.' The other: 'Just had a successful cancer operation, Jack. Come and see me.' The second telegram was the one which was despatched.

I have described Haldane as a secular saint. Some people might accuse me of reducing a rich personality to a mere type. They might quote Scott Fitzgerald's dictum: 'Create an individual and you create a type; create a type and you have nothing.' But Haldane is not from fiction. His personality transcended fictional types and defied classification. In his complex character incompatible elements struggled for some sort of synthesis. Most striking was the reduction of a great deal of objective and materialistic science into an intensely individual and even humane

*See 'On Being Finite' published in *The Rationalist Annual*, edited by Hector Hawton.

personality. I was pleased that after his death I was invited to write a short appreciation of him for the *Manchester Guardian*. One learns from one's seniors how to do many things – and how not to do them.

6

The Lure of the New World

As a refugee in Britain I was luckier than most *émigrés*. To me it often seemed more like a return than an emigration, for the kind of society I found in London and Harpenden was not unlike that which had been cherished at home before the terrible flood of Nazism engulfed everything. I had been fortunate too that I had never personally encountered the worst excesses of this cataclysmic regime. But I was not sympathetic to the post-war hysteria of those who advocated the abolition of the German language, or vowed that they would never again listen to a piece of music by Wagner.

As a scientist I believed that I had a broader approach to biology than my new colleagues. In Britain I observed a curious emphasis on Darwinism and evolution; for myself I was always more interested in how organisms work and how ecological ambiences co-operate than in speculating as to how it all came about. To the Anglo-Saxons the German scientific tradition is seen as pedantic, philosophical, metaphysical and abstruse; the German scholars consider the British to be pragmatic and unwilling or unable – possibly both – to indulge in philosophical considerations. Anyway, to me the preoccupation with Darwinism was highly fanciful and not pragmatic at all, although when the British are pragmatic, I find them delightful. As an example I will relate a case history, which is typical of the way in which the British deal with eccentrics. Amongst the scholarly immigrants was a young palaeontologist from Berlin, later a professor in that same city, whose forte it was to find new sites of fossils. When war broke out and foreign nationals were forbidden to possess maps, he continued to explore the countryside, entering the locations of his discoveries on large-scale maps. Eventually he was arrested and spent most of the war in a camp on the Isle of Man. Professor D.M.S. Watson, in whose department he had been working, was unable to obtain his release, but the prisoner was allowed to receive a microscope and large quantities of rocks from one of his sites. From these he was able to extract a new species of Jurassic mammal, and to complete his doctoral thesis.

The end of the war brought new dislocations to the lives of some exiles. University College had been reassembled some months before and the long and laborious years of reconstruction had begun. The common experiences of the war years had brought exiles and hosts closer to each other, and coping with the straitened financial circumstances, the slow-moving social changes, the loss of Empire and the search for a new role in the world, was also a shared experience. Exiles ceased to think of themselves as foreigners. Most of them acquired British nationality. They had never conspicuously formed themselves into a separate group, and now their work became increasingly integrated into the life of the College.

There were refugees – notably Hungarians – who seemed 'pre-adapted' to English ways and were to achieve considerable prominence in Britain. Others were less adaptable. For instance, the son of a famous professor in my home university, was born in Oxford while his parents were visiting the university town, and thus, as a British subject, had no difficulty in entering this country. However, he had considerable difficulty with the language. He was taken in by some old colleagues of his father and set out daily to the Bodleian Library in pursuit of some oriental studies. After a few months his protectors provided him with a small grant and set him up in digs. They did all they could to help him adjust to English ways, including ordering meals in restaurants. When he enquired what he should order, the friends suggested fish and chips. This worked well until after a while he complained that it was getting monotonous. What else could he order? 'Steak,' was the suggestion and he wrote the word in his diary. The following day in his usual restaurant he ordered 'steak', and the waiter enquired did he want his steak rare, medium, or well done? Quite at a loss he could only repeat that what he wanted was 'steak'. After some confusion he resigned himself to his fate and, returning to the established routine, feebly demanded 'feesh and cheeps'.

At the time of my arrival in Britain and for many years thereafter I was aware of Britain's world-wide imperial connections. Having felt myself initially rather like a Greek who had escaped from messy political involvements at home to the less imaginative but more orderly Roman world – England – I came to regard myself as more like a latter-day British imperialist visiting distant outposts of the Empire. Even when the colonies became dominions or republics, I observed little difference in attitudes, and when I travelled I pictured myself as a monk in the Middle Ages receiving hospitality and debating points of common interest all over the known world.

Having done war work for the Navy and boasting no particular political affiliations I had no difficulties with the naturalisation procedures and was one of the first applicants to be granted British citizenship, as a result of which my sons were automatically British too. Nussy had to apply separately and was granted her citizenship a few weeks later. By the time my brother, Ernst, who had left Czechoslovakia on skis and who had endured numerous adventures before reaching England, applied some years afterwards things had become a good deal less straightforward. To his astonishment the detective interviewing him was much more interested in me than in him, and concentrated mainly on my having worked in Haldane's department which he found incomprehensible. That my brother had for some time been fighting in the Czech army under Soviet command the detective thought altogether less important. On the whole I concluded that my file must have been compiled with the help of American intelligence.

Our first Christmas in London was a sad affair. My right eye was afflicted with one of my regular bouts of corneal herpes, a condition which had been incompetently treated in Moorfields Hospital. With my head bandaged I would walk over Hampstead Heath to the underground station, travel in overcrowded trains, shiver in draughty tunnels and on escalators, wait interminably on long benches for doctors or nurses. There had been a sharp frost, followed by a sudden thaw, as a result of which a pipe burst under our roof. We had never known such a thing before coming to Britain. In the morning our staircase was bedecked with ice and icicles decorated the banisters. Despite these inconveniences Nussy tried to prepare a Christmas Eve supper, such as we had enjoyed in Prague. This would consist of fish soup followed by roast carp. As the English do not eat carp, Nussy had to travel to the East End where she found in a Jewish shop a rather small carp, a very poor relation to the huge beasts which had spent their last days in our Prague bath-tub. To keep it fresh she left the carp in the outdoor coal-shed. But when she went to fetch it she found only the wrapping paper and a few bones, abandoned by the neighbour's cat. The mainstay of our feast that year was sardines. The boys' stockings were also sadly depleted, a few small items from Woolworths being all that we could manage. But at least there was a tree, and a piano with which to accompany our singing.

My eyes had troubled me since my early university days. I have suffered more than 30 episodes of corneal herpes despite treatment by some of the most illustrious opthalmologists in Europe, many of whom I knew personally through a common interest in colour blindness. I have never been able to ascertain what provoked the eruption of the herpes, which appears to lurk permanently in some eye ganglion, nor why it mostly affected the lids and only occasionally the cornea. I was treated surgically and with drugs, both in hospital and at home; nothing made much difference. In later years some of the modern anti-viral drugs seemed to speed up the recovery, but unfortunately my vision deteriorated with every attack, so that latterly I could neither do fine work over the microscope, nor read for more than an hour or two at a time, and never in poor light. This Damoclean sword which has been hanging over my head now for over 60 years has ruled out clinical pursuits and other occupations which require freedom from interruption, so that I never became a practising doctor. Travel to remote places always involved some risk, although I only twice suffered attacks while away from home.

There was a positive side to all this. My unique situation – the combination of my personal deficiency and my familiarity with the methods of exploring subjective visual phenomena – enabled me to observe some peculiarities in dark adaptation, colour and double vision, which had not been described before.

Despite the humiliations after the war there were offers, and some very tempting ones. My problem was which to choose. There was a proposal that I might accept a chair of zoology in one of the German universities, perhaps in Berlin. The West German government had awarded me a compensatory pension and the rank of professor. The idea of regenerating German biology greatly appealed to me, but it would have meant a second emigration to a new country, for I had never lived in Germany, only visited that country. Nussy was unwilling to go, and the boys would have had to change the language in which they were being educated. Furthermore the miserable conditions in Germany immediately after the war and doubts about the persistence of the Nazi ideology were discouraging factors. I said no.

Then there was an invitation to return to Prague. My love for my home town was, and is, undiminished, but I could not see myself working whole-heartedly in a Czech and Communist university. It would be a return all right, but a return to a cemetery. Another offer came from the Hebrew University of Jerusalem, where I had given a course in human genetics and a series of lectures on the behaviour of the honey-bee. I was asked whether they should establish a chair of genetics and whether I would accept it, if offered. I wrote back, arguing against the establishment of a separate chair of genetics; as to whether I would wish to become its first incumbent, if one were to be established, I was touched by the offer, but was not prepared to learn enough Hebrew to become a university lecturer; besides which I had been brought up a Protestant.

After teaching a genetics course at the summer school in the University at Bloomington, Indiana, Tracy Sonneborn suggested to the medical school, in the sister medical faculty in Indianapolis, that a human genetics department might be created for me. Nothing came of this, which maybe was just as well because shortly afterwards I was declared a 'prohibited immigrant' by the US authorities.

The most tempting offer came from my friend, the Zurich zoologist, Ernst Hadorn. He asked me to take the chair of anthropology at his home university. I would once again be speaking my mother tongue, and my beloved mountains would be within easy reach, but I was still concerned that my wife and children would be uprooted. Nussy made it clear that she had no desire to be a 'Frau Professor'.

It was gratifying to be in demand from the Germans, the Czechs, the Israelis and the Swiss, but I only considered one offer to be a serious possibility.

Late in the summer of 1949 Nussy brought a telegram to the local hospital where I lay recovering from a bout of my recurrent eye trouble. It was an invitation to become Associate Professor of Genetics at McGill University in Montreal. I thought long and hard.

London University was the largest in the Commonwealth and the mother of many smaller colleges scattered throughout the world. The opportunities to teach and to initiate research were considerable there, and the Galton Laboratory, at which I was working, was the foremost institution at which to study human genetics. It played host to almost all the important visiting workers in the field. The younger ones became the founders of schools of their own in numerous countries. Reciprocal visits were easily arranged. But my chances for promotion did not seem too good and Professor Penrose, my immediate chief at that time, advised me to accept the offer. He told Nussy that, as an immigrant, I would be more acceptable in Canada, where a large percentage of the population had recently arrived, than in England, where my foreign origins and education would always remain an impediment. If this remark had been intended to encourage me to make a permanent break with University College, it had the opposite effect. It made me realise, however, that once away from England I might find it difficult to return to the academic establishment, should I not like Canada or McGill. Although at that time England did not seem too hospitable, Canada seemed like deportation.

But it was not my first opportunity of working in Canada. During my first month in England G.P. Wells had suggested that I might wish to take a post in Toronto, but after I showed some initial reluctance the idea was dropped. The boat which would have taken us across the Atlantic was torpedoed. Another offer had reached me via Professor Penrose when McGill's Department of Genetics was looking for an assistant professor to teach biometry. But the salary of 3,000 dollars would have been barely enough to keep a family and so I had declined.

I certainly did not want to burn my bridges, but would have been foolish to have ignored Penrose's advice. So I decided, after talking things over with Nussy and the boys, to take a year's unpaid leave from London and accept the professorship in Montreal working under Professor Boyes. For the time being Nussy and the children would remain in Hertfordshire.

I wrote to Haldane and requested leave, adding that I would be away only for a year. I do not think anyone believed me. A Canadian colleague accompanied me to the Canadian High Commission, where the officials were extremely friendly, and despite my eye trouble (my head was encased in bandages) I was granted the necessary exit visa.

I left Harpenden on 4 October and sailed on the *Aquitania*, an old Cunarder which had been a troopship during the war and had only just been refitted for civilian use. Six tugs dragged us from the Southampton pier, and as we sailed we passed the *Mauretania* and the lit up *Queen Mary*. Dinner was excellent and I shared a table with a Liverpool industrialist and his wife and a mining engineer from Nova Scotia. Afterwards there were bagpipes and moonshine and when I retired to my 'stateroom and bath', I found myself sharing with five other passengers including a Bible-reading Canadian farmer, a Socialist photographer and an electrician from the Midlands.

Life aboard the *Aquitania* was a welcome holiday. There were enormous breakfasts and salt-water baths. Amongst the passengers was a professor from Pisa who was on his way with his family to McGill for his second year teaching philosophy, and who told me many details about the life I would be leading.

Observing the first-class passengers, I was immediately struck by the contrast between the 'society' and the jobless emigrants from all over Europe. The Dowager Countess of Lucan, alleged mother-in-law of Lord Alexander, the Canadian High Commissioner, asked me to teach her deck-tennis; I played too much shuffle-board and was punished with a sore shoulder.

My first night in Montreal, which was enjoying a heat-wave, was spent at the Faculty Club, where I slept in a sham-Gothic turret room, linked through an archway to a gigantic billiards room. My first experience of the McGill campus was favourable. Professor Boyes took me to his home and introduced me to his hefty wife and four sturdy and completely uninhibited children. They played happily in the corner of the sitting-room while a maid brought in the drinks. After watching their game for a while I was amused to observe that it was a version of 'Doctors and Nurses'. It consisted of a girl putting a pillow under her petticoat and the boy rather forcibly removing it. To my mind it was really the most harmless of games, but the maid, a French-speaking Catholic, who had only entered service with the family the previous day found such recreations revolting and immediately gave in her notice, saying that she couldn't possibly serve in such a heathen household.

There were a number of journalists, both French and English, waiting for me and wanting to know what I intended to do at McGill. Unused to reporters I told them brusquely to leave me alone and go away. In the corridor they met the head of the department and complained to him, whereupon he assured me that it was absolutely essential for the prestige of McGill that I deal accommodatingly with the press. After this they all trooped back into my room to continue with their questions. I took refuge in scientific jargon, but they persisted in asking me directly what it was I actually proposed to do. I was interested at that time in trying to find a link between the A, B and O blood groups and red hair, and I told them this, with the result that they all volunteered to find me families with a high incidence of red-heads. When they returned with a handful of red-heads they had not thought to bring with them any non-red-headed siblings, and so the whole procedure was a waste of time, but nevertheless I pricked the girls' fingers. Photographs were circulated throughout the entire Canadian and North American press, and for several years I was known as the chap who bled beautiful red-heads. I used to send cuttings home with a careful explanation, lest my family jumped to the wrong conclusions.

I explored the campus and the city, noting that although children were not allowed to visit the cinema until they were 16, they could marry at 14. I was amazed in a low den off St Catherine's Street to be served soup, rollmops and a full pound weight of red steak. I was relieved in my first letter from Nussy to hear that, so long as my children stayed in England, I should be almost completely tax-exempted.

I found teaching the elements of biometry not particularly arduous, the greatest difficulty being that the biologists and medical students in my classes were almost innumerate and encountered considerable problems in understanding even the simplest algebraic formulae. One of the lecturers in the mathematics department took a cynical view of my 20-hour course and reckoned that he could have dealt with it in about a quarter of an hour. But I believe that my thoroughness was useful to my students, although I was disappointed at the results of the examination which I set them myself. There was one curious misunderstanding which I put down to the strangeness of my accent for Americans and Canadians. I dictated some of the questions, one of which was to name the cytological equivalent of the genetical phenomenon of crossing-over. Most of the students gave the correct answer (chiasma) but about half-a-dozen said it was schizophrenia. I was bewildered as to how anybody could give such an answer, until I realised that they must have misheard cytology for psychology.

Genetics was a compulsory subject for biologists and medics, and optional for many other students, including nurses, physio-therapists, educationalists and the like. Consequently classes were crowded, both the lectures and the practicals, which were held in four parallel classes on four weekday afternoons. It seemed to me fatuous. Where was the sense in teaching future nurses *Drosophila* techniques? There were too few of us to supervise the classes satisfactorily, which became chaotic, the flies escaped before they could be counted and nobody had the faintest idea what to do with their results.

A few weeks before Christmas Professor Boyes invited me to a congress organised by the American Genetical Society in New York and scheduled for 28 December. I was keen to accept, particularly as it would be my first visit to New York.

Christmas separated from my wife and children was a rather sad and solitary experience, despite the generous hospitality from several quarters. Christmas Eve I spent with Professor Mackintosh and his family and helped fill the stockings of his four daughters. Christmas Day was spent at the Boyes house where I helped to demolish an enormous turkey and played with the children. I had already sent my family presents, English-made goods, including a large tin of assorted biscuits, which were readily available in Montreal although not at home. In return I had received from Harpenden John Gunther's book *Inside the USA*, a pair of skiing mittens, an alpine calendar, a diary, and some quince cheese.

Wally Boyes and I travelled by train and approached New York on a cold December morning. Instead of the famous view of the skyline of Manhattan seen from on board a great liner, our first sight of the city was a dingy, sooty railway station. In the hotel in which the Triple A congress was being held I was amazed at the vast number of scientists and the general air of heightened activity.

During the sessions and between them I was introduced to many of the leading American geneticists, and renewed my friendship with some old colleagues and acquaintances. I also gave two short lectures which were well attended.

The high point of the trip was a lecture given by Herman J. Muller, who had just received the Nobel Prize for his production of mutants by X-rays in *Drosophila*. Though a most sympathetic man, he was a very poor lecturer, and towards the end of his 90-minute presentation he became entangled in a formula for the results of mutation rates in which he hesitated for quite a while over whether to put a number above or below the division line – and this in front of many representatives of the international press.

There was not enough time. I ate at a delicatessen on Broadway and strolled across Central Park at night, walking home via Columbus Circle, Times Square and Seventh Avenue to my hotel. The lights were spectacular and the throngs of people seemed happy, though there were many sleeping on pavements. I took the ferry (five cents) to Staten Island past the Statue of Liberty. I walked along Wall Street, and at the Museum of Natural History I was much impressed by the huge exhibits. Also present in the enormous halls were some 3,000 people, drinking beer from tins, Coca Cola from bottles. I took a trip on a train called 'The Twilight' to visit my friend, Ernst Hock, and his father – our father's old schoolmaster, Dr Hock, 81 years old and still working on his book on *Genius*. I stayed with them in the Appalachians for several days, and talked with Dr Hock on politics, neurology, the National Health Service and the Catholic Church. In between times we listened to Beethoven, Negro Spirituals, Czech folk-songs, Lohengrin broadcast from the Metropolitan and looked at a magnificent picture-book of Prague and the Hock home movies. And then I returned to McGill. The day after my return was my 44th birthday. In my diary is the cryptic entry: 'Feel young and old at the same time.'

Before making a final decision about the future I thought that Nussy should come over and have a look at Canada for herself. She arrived in May, sailing up the St Lawrence in some of the most violent storms for years. Concerned lest she were put off by my accommodation in rather dingy student quarters – I had not minded leading the life of an impecunious student when I was alone – I had my secretary rent me a rather better apartment a little way up the mountain. On my first evening there – Nussy was due to arrive the following morning – after a convivial party given by the Professors of Medicine and Dermatology, I arrived back at my new flat rather late at night. Having undressed I made for the bathroom, but the door slammed behind me and locked me out, leaving me on the staircase in my pyjamas in a house in which I was quite unknown. What made an awkward situation worse was that there were only a few hours to go before I had to get ready to meet Nussy on the pier where the steamer from London docked at some unearthly hour. An old lady on her way to the lavatory met me on the stairs, and I had the greatest difficulty in persuading her not to call the police.

In Montreal Nussy had her first T-bone steak. In May I took her on a visit to New York. But I think we had both come to realise that our future was to be in England. As the children turned into adults and carved out successful careers in the academic world and in medicine, I was to find myself increasingly concerned with local institutions. I continued to teach at University College, and became chairman of this and committee member of that.

My original plans for the summer had been to test the Canadian Indians and possibly some Eskimos for the PTC tasting factor; also to take some blood from them to discover whether they had positive antigens in their red blood cells. I had prepared these field trips carefully, getting permission from the Mounties to ride out with them to remote areas where they were paying out the annual treaty money, as a consequence of the treaties of the early settlers with the Indians. But money was running short and I changed my plans. I would get a summer job, very much the tradition in American academic circles. After some enquiries I landed a lectureship for the summer term at Bloomington, Indiana.

At Bloomington I was required to give a great many lectures, but there were no practicals and, as the work was low grade, I did not find it too demanding. I lived a short distance from the campus, and walked to work every morning. I think I was the only one in my class who did. The campus was set in a semi-tropical park with the institutional buildings well scattered. It was hot in the summer and the only room in my department which was air-conditioned was the fly-room, so that was where I spent a good deal of my time. Many of the professors lived in the old homesteads built by the original settlers. In the vicinity were numerous ponds, dug, I was told, during the summer famine years in the last century to provide labour for the unemployed. In some of these I would swim with Mrs Sonneborn and some friends of hers, but the most spectacular places to swim were the deserted quarries, from which had been taken the stone for most of the monumental buildings in Washington. I was reminded of ancient Greece with the drums of Doric columns, broken architraves, and other elements of classical architecture. The water was a deep green and clean, and in it, to my joyous surprise, were thousands of the freshwater medusa, *Cruspida*, a very rare animal which appears epidemically in temperate zones and which I had only seen once before in Bohemia. These quarries had been closed to the public, but Professor Horowitz, a biochemist from Prague, and his family, were skilled trespassers and we had some wonderful summer swimming at the weekends.

I had time to do some work of my own and, while I could have worked with Sonneborn on some *Paramecium* problem, this organism having been the subject of my first monograph, I decided to undertake some mutation work with some of the famous trick stocks of *Drosophila* developed by Herman Muller. Specifically I wanted to test whether the absence of oxygen during irradiation, which decreases the number of radiation-induced mutations, was caused by the physical absence of oxygen or only by the inability to use oxygen in some metabolic process. My plan was to anaesthetise the fruit-flies either with hydrocyanic acid or with another agent which would block the oxygen available for metabolism, and then irradiate the flies and count the mutants. I found that the mutation rate *was* reduced and that the reduction was due to the blockage of oxygen for metabolic purposes rather than to the absence of oxygen in the air, because oxygen was, of course, present during these kinds of irradiations.

I suggested to Muller that I might use Muller 5, one of his famous stocks, but he insisted that he had something very much better which would save me one generation and ensure that I achieved many more results in the few weeks available to me. I started to multiply the new trick stock with the help of one of the students who carefully explained to me how it worked. The results of my first experiments appeared to be sensational, the mutation rate being reduced drastically by the presence of cyanide or azide, and both Muller and Sonneborn became highly excited, insisting that I should pursue these kinds of experiments and even reporting my results to Oakland, the big research centre. But when I tried to repeat my experiments, disaster struck. The stock began to disintegrate and in the limited time available to me I was quite unable to produce any further reasonable results. So I had to abandon that promising line of research and it was only many years later that experiments of this kind were continued elsewhere, and the results I had obtained from my first batch of stock were confirmed.

While in Bloomington I received a letter from an old physicist friend of mine from Prague who had become Professor of Physics at the University of Arkansas in Fayetteville. He was eager to find me a job in the Zoology Department. Sonneborn and Muller insisted that no one in his senses would go to such a place, but when I received a second and very insistent letter with the money for the journey I decided to take a look. Fayetteville was beautiful and the visit intriguing. The University seemed to be segregated; at least there were no black people to be seen. The interviewing committee was oafish, and I realised why my Bloomington colleagues had been so scathing. I must admit to having been tempted by the excellent salary I was offered, but I resisted. However, the days I spent there enabled me to gain some insight into southern society and I thought the Blue Ridge area beautiful.

Despite all these diversions and some quite intensive work I became lonely in Bloomington and glad when the time came for me to return to Montreal. In due course I was going to have to decide whether to bring the family over and settle there, but as time passed the arguments against doing so seemed to grow stronger. I thought the personnel mixed and the intellectual standards not quite as high as I had expected. More seriously the national tensions between the French and English speakers in the province of Quebec forcibly reminded me of similarities with the Germans and Czechs in Bohemia. Would it have been fair to my family, having removed them from one contentious country, to have settled them in another? My colleagues at McGill ridiculed me for these concerns, but the tensions have not lessened and the nationalists amongst the French speakers have certainly made life in the province uncomfortable for the English Canadians.

I left McGill and Montreal and Canada in August 1950. Nussy and the children met me at Euston. Together we went home.

7

Remarkable Men

I have lived and worked with many remarkable men, besides Professor Haldane, and I have been exposed to many others.

Albert Einstein had been Professor of Theoretical Physics at my Prague University. Although I did not attend the lectures he gave for the physicists of both universities, I did go to a couple of public disputations, chaired by Einstein's successor, Philip Frank. In these Einstein was opposed by Oscar Kraus, a philosopher who was also a friend of my parents. He is best remembered for a humorous epic called *Schlarafia*, which deals with his class-mates, including my father, and is a classic of German literature. I also remember him as the author of a play in which the members of our university appear in the guise of Athenian philosophers.

However, despite Kraus's undoubted wit, talent and imagination, the disputations were very one-sided. Philip Frank chaired the proceedings with characteristic sarcasm, but there was not the slightest doubt about the superiority and clarity of Einstein's arguments. In person he made an exceptionally pleasing impression. Handsome and mild mannered, he seemed to be in a state of what I can best describe as lyricism. None the less when I attended a concert in which he played the violin, I have to say that his playing was decidedly unlyrical! I had already been deeply shocked by Einstein's Theory of Relativity, so the disputations revealed nothing unfamiliar to me. But one could not be in Einstein's presence without being aware of the intellect and *niceness* of the man.

A colleague of mine at the University of Prague was Kurt Sitte. He lectured in physics, I in zoology. And we were rivals on the track, both being sprinters; I usually won our races by a short head. A social democrat and married to a Jewish girl, Sitte was violently anti-Hitler. He worked in some physics laboratories in America, where he was removed from top secret work, but emigrated to Israel where he undertook important experiments in fusion. But he could not shake off his old Communist affiliations, and he was blackmailed into giving secrets of Israeli research to the Soviets. He was found out and put on trial. The Israeli authorities took into account his great achievements and the valuable contribution he had made to Israeli physics, and his sentence was only a few years in prison. I believe that he is now a professor at an East German university.

In Haldane's department at London University were several remarkable men and women, and one of the most remarkable was Hans Gruneberg. A refugee from Germany he later became a very eminent geneticist and Fellow of the Royal Society. Spending many years in the same department a curious friendship grew up between us.

He had been brought up strictly in the Prussian tradition. A rigid disciplinarian, he organised himself with single-mindedness, and tied up all the loose ends in his academic work. He treated his people with harsh paternalistic authority and drilled them thoroughly. As a result they all landed good jobs and usually owed their distinguished careers to him. Towards the end of his life he told me repeatedly that he had finished every piece of work that he had started and would leave no unfinished projects behind him. This of course was not literally true, because, like every good scientist he asked more questions than he answered, but he had not spent – or, as he would have put it – wasted any time on sidelines. I could not help but compare his technique with mine, as I remembered my steel cabinets crammed with unfinished or half-finished work, some of it no more than jottings.

I have always had many more ideas than I could possibly cope with and I have never been able properly to control what I should be doing next. Had I been in charge of a research group such haphazardness would have been disastrously inefficient, but working, as I usually have, on my own, I do not believe that my work has suffered. The urge to branch out in all directions has kept me alert and enabled me to dabble in numerous things which I would not otherwise have been concerned about.

I have sometimes been too quick to publish results and conclusions, but often when I have delayed I have been anticipated by others working in the same field. One example is the use of deuterium oxide (heavy water) instead of water to slow down the endogenous rhythm of various organisms, for instance the eclosion (hatching) of *Drosophila*. I never published my experiments which more or less confirmed those of Pittendrigh.

In old age I am never short of a project. All I have to do is turn to my cabinets and folders and browse for a while. I can be certain of turning up something which has been lying about for years but which is still sufficiently relevant to contemporary problems to make it worth pursuing.

I believe that the ideas I have about self-discipline apply equally to the organisation of societies. Strict controls have some desirable short-term effects, no doubt, but they deaden individual development and hinder the natural evolution of our institutions. The answer is that discipline should be internal, each person should control his or her own behaviour to the maxims which he or she has formulated. As someone matures the process is to internalise disciplines imposed from without. Sadly, in most societies very few people are free to control their own destinies in this way; sadly, also, the emphasis is too often on performance and too little on intellectual and academic introspection.

The greatest achievement of the highly disciplined Gruneberg was a study of pleotropism, specifically the multifarious manifestation of mutants in mice, which he considered the model organism for human hereditary pathology. He wrote a number of papers and two remarkable books on the subject. Considering the detailed analysis of the morphological effects of the mutants he described, it was strange how clumsy he was – a clumsiness he shared with Haldane incidentally – and how totally dependent upon the manipulations of his technicians. He could delegate work to his research students, but was psychologically incapable of collaboration on equal terms. If I suggested such a collaboration, he would become agitated and irrational; I believe there was a repressed fear or uncertainty which prevented him working equally with a colleague. From one of his hobbies I profited greatly. He had a love for India and Indian architecture which had grown out of long periods of research and travel in that country, and when I told him that Nussy and I were planning a prolonged journey through India and Ceylon, he became hugely enthusiastic and prepared a detailed three-month itinerary for us, writing numerous letters of introduction and ensuring that our trip would be a pleasurable one.

Among the many colourful personalities who visited our laboratory the most remarkable may well have been Norbert Wiener, the inventor of cybernetics, or, if not the inventor, at least the man who gave this branch of science its name.

One morning while I was doing some calculations, Haldane appeared with a small, thickset man with a little goatee beard and the powerful glasses which indicated myopia. The newcomer planted himself in front of me while Haldane introduced us and added: 'Kalmus is interested in periodicity.'

At once Wiener got hold of a piece of chalk and proceeded to cover a huge blackboard on the wall of my room with integral signs and a great variety of symbols, the entire activity being conducted in silence. As soon as he had completed his business he looked rather forlorn and stared for a while into the air, then bowed politely to me and left the room with Haldane. Together with my colleagues we spent a while trying to puzzle out what had been written on the blackboard, but could find no connection with periodicity at all. I photographed the blackboard but it remains a mystery to this day.

Numerous anecdotes, many of them malicious, circulated about Wiener. It was frequently alleged that the trees near his Institute had to be replanted because he always drove his car into them. He was renowned for being totally absorbed in his thoughts and totally unaware of his environment. It was said that one morning his wife announced to him that they had moved the previous night and, since she was only too aware of his helplessness and forgetfulness, she handed him a piece of paper with their new address on it. Later that day Wiener wandering aimlessly about planted himself in front of a passing child and said: 'My child, I am Professor Norbert Wiener, can you tell me where I live?' To which the child replied: 'But yes, Dad. Mum has just sent me out to look for you!'

On another occasion as he was leaving the Institute he met a student and they began talking shop, going to and fro along the block. When they came to the end of their conversation Wiener asked the student: 'Was I going south or north when we met?' 'North,' said the student. 'Then,' said Wiener, 'I have not yet had lunch.'

Wiener's behaviour and appearance seemed appropriate to his chosen subject, automatic mechanisms and artificial intelligence devices. In his presence I could not but be reminded of the mythical figure of the Prague Golem, invented by the rabbis in the Middle Ages as a sort of mechanical homuncule of the ghetto. He was indeed an extreme example of what was known as 'the polarised mind', namely a mind attuned only to impressions connected with the job in hand and impervious to everything else. There is an example nearer home which has caused my family a good deal of amusement.

Peter, my elder son, once gave a lecture at a meeting of the Physical Society and afterwards a colleague approached him and asked him whether he might be related to a man called Kalmus whom he used to know. Peter obviously thought that this man must be referring to his brother, George, who is also a physicist, but the other man shook his head and said that it could not have been his brother, it must have been a much older man. Upon which Peter asked whether perhaps he remembered the name of his acquaintance. 'Yes,' was the reply after a moment's hesitation, 'I think he was called Hans.' 'Never heard of him,' said Peter, but then added: 'On second thoughts – I think that is my father!'

I take some satisfaction in the clear evidence that I have certainly not overawed my children.

There was never much doubt that they would become scientists, the leading question being which discipline they would favour. Both my sons had exceedingly good physics and mathematics teachers at the grammar school in St Albans, but at that time it was not usually possible for pupils to learn biology as well as the exact sciences, so the boys settled for physics, and it may have been a wise choice because both became professors. My daughter, who was much younger, did not benefit at school from the influence of any particularly charismatic teacher, and therefore had a more difficult choice to make. But the family's medical tradition combined with a powerful social conscience persuaded her to become a doctor.

Despite having gone to school without interruption for more than 70 years, I do not overestimate the importance of formal education. Nussy never went to any school, but was taught by rather mediocre tutors at home before spending a year at a finishing school in Paris. It was the Victorian attitude of her parents who sent the three boys to university but kept the girls at home. However, Nussy speaks more languages than I, and I do not believe that her intellect has been stunted by not sitting on a school bench. Some disciplines she lacked; she received no formal instruction in mathematics, but her sums are more accurate than mine and she can do them more quickly. But she cannot properly understand what her two physicist sons are up to, nor her mathematician grandson – to tell the absolute truth, no more can I!

Nussy and I had long contemplated the acquisition of some small holiday home. Naturally I had in mind some small chalet in the Alps, but Nussy tended rather to the Mediterranean. Then one day in the University common-room I was casually leafing through an edition of *Country Life* when I came across a small advertisement offering 'two small cottages of character' in a place near Tintagel at a modest price. That same afternoon we went to tea with our friends, Professor Gregory and his wife, who we discovered had similar ideas to our own. It was not long before we jointly purchased the pair of miners' cottages, and we have been enjoying their amenities ever since.

I found the west country a most magical place to live, the wild Atlantic, the splendid views from the beaches, the cliffs, the valleys and the moors, the huge churches isolated from any centres of population, the fishing and the quarrying; it would have been impossible to have found a greater or more restful contrast to university life.

But I never could quite get away from my profession. In a Cornish house adjacent to ours there lived a child who suffered from phenylkytenuria. I prescribed the restricted diet which prevents this metabolic disability from degenerating into feeble-mindedness, and the child is now a healthy and fully active adult.

In this case I was certainly of use, but there were other occasions on which I was able to save lives – and not only in my capacity as a doctor. The first such was when I was walking with a friend on the lower quayside along the River Moldau. It was a fine evening, and the upper level was crowded, but the lower more or less deserted. Suddenly we noticed an agitated young woman, some yards upstream of where we were standing. She was in tears and to our horror she ran towards the water and jumped in, fully dressed, with handbag and umbrella. We assumed that it was a suicide attempt, but she started to shout for help as she bobbed about, now under, now above the water. There was a boat chained to a ring in the quay wall from which we might reach the woman without immersing ourselves; we climbed in and released it. As we reached the woman I leant overboard while my friend sat on my legs. I dragged her into the boat and we deposited her on the quayside, then hurriedly disappeared before the people from the upper level could get down. I remember feeling some satisfaction, not so much that I had saved a life, but that I had saved my father one more post-mortem.

On another occasion I was climbing with my brother in the Yugoslavian Alps. We were roped together and crossing a steep gully with some caution because we knew the rocks to be unstable. All at once I heard a rumble from above and glanced up to see some boulders hurtling towards us. I pressed instantly forward to the very edge of the gully, pulling my brother off the path. Although he cursed loudly he forgave me when he saw huge boulders bouncing across the path where a moment before we had been standing.

In collaboration with a Brazilian colleague I was studying some Indian settlements near the Argentine border. It was bitterly cold, the tree ferns around us were covered with frost, and the Indians assembled in the small schoolhouse were shivering. I had just taken some blood samples from a young couple when I noticed that the woman had a young child in a sling on her back and that the child was whimpering. I called the woman back and asked what was wrong with the child, diagnosing a serious attack of whooping cough with a high temperature. Fortunately we had some vaccine with us and were able to inject the child. I also insisted that the family spend the night indoors near the fire, and in the morning the patient was much improved. A bow and arrows which the father brought me in gratitude a day later still hang in my hall.

There have also been occasions on which I narrowly escaped death. Once I was diving into what I thought was the clear water of the Danube. I landed, pelvis first, on a post. Having torn my bathing suit I crawled out of the water and asked some onlookers to bring me a towel. While they were doing so I fainted and rolled into the muddy water. It appears that I was later fished out and revived.

While that was an accident, there have been occasions when it seems that I deliberately courted trouble. I was on holiday with my Carinthian relatives. I must have been about 16 and rather too full of myself as a result of which I was teased a good deal by two girl cousins, who were both a little older than I. Having mentioned that I had done some boxing they challenged me to a bout with a friend of theirs who was also a boxer. I readily agreed to be confronted by a burly young man, a medical student some five years older than myself, and champion of his university. He glanced at my weedy physique and remarked that it was clearly a mismatch but the girls giggled and egged us both on. We put on the gloves and started to spar. To begin with he was content to let me do the attacking and merely defend himself, but after I penetrated his guard he went on the attack and I came to, lying in the grass with my face being washed with cold water.

At about the same time I had an even more ludicrous adventure which for some reason sticks in my memory. There lived in Prague a highly eccentric lady, the wife of a colleague of my father's. She came from a very rich banking family in Vienna, and had been brought up by English governesses from whom she had acquired a number of idiosyncrasies. She aped the British upper classes in one respect at least; she always looked exceedingly dowdy and her huge flat was in permanent chaos. She never visited a hairdresser or tailor and merely ordered her wardrobe each year by saying: 'The same as last time.' She was notorious in the streets of Prague, and could have been mistaken for a member of the Salvation Army with her curious poke bonnet, her heavy boots and an unidentifiable uniform. All this topped by pince-nez hanging on a huge hooked nose. Although she was highly intelligent, her political ideas were as bizarre as her appearance, for she was a confirmed Hapsburg monarchist.

Becoming interested in geology she and several of her children joined me on a fossil-hunt a few miles from town. On the return journey we were walking towards the river bank whence we would take the ferry when we were passed by a series of motor cars which raised the dust; and the dust penetrated our eyes and noses. I grew so annoyed that I collected some spittle in my mouth and spat it at the next approaching car. It stopped. Out stepped a huge chauffeur whose manner was by no means conciliatory. I looked first at him, and then at the geological hammer which I was still carrying, and so for a short while we stood, facing each other, to the astonishment and embarrassment of my companions. The travellers in the car, members of another rich Prague family, were also acquaintances of the lady accompanying me, and had of course recognised her. They called off their chauffeur, and I was able to laugh heartily at the encounter. I believe that I was taken for one of the social revolutionaries, commonly seen at that time in and around Prague. I was not so much protesting against the rich, however, as showing my disapproval of having to walk through clouds of dust.

In spite of the experience of persecution which I share with millions of less fortunate contemporaries from Central Europe, I seem to be incapable of sustained or personal hatred. My attitude is similar to that of the Chicago gangsters who used to proclaim: 'Don't get mad, get even.' Dislike is as much as I can manage and this is directed not so much against individuals as against certain types of people and the misconceptions they hold. Consequently I have often found myself involved with a motley assortment of people united only by their common enemies. Before and during the early days of the Second World War I found myself amongst Utopians, Communists, anarchists, and even patriots with whom I had thought to find common cause although on closer analysis it appeared that we were unlikely to agree, and I very soon left them to their own devices.

When I compare myself to others I find that I seldom abandon myself to excesses of love or affection, any more than to hatred. I have been described as 'a cold fish'. But I reject this judgement. Looking at myself I find a curious dichotomy. In theoretical matters I would certainly agree with Spinoza who considered the *amours des intellectuelles* to be the highest form of curiosity, which in modern terms means that one has to think about everything there is and reject nothing as unthinkable. Spinoza also disapproved of emotions of all kinds. Although in practical and intellectual matters I am almost compulsively detached, I would not take Spinoza's extreme position. Emotions are necessary to fire the intellectual engine, but they can become so strong that they cloud the mind and act against sober and systematic procedures. Certainly this is the case where sexual emotions are concerned. Research can best be done in the comparative peace of a good marriage, or by divorcing animal instincts from personal involvements – a practice popular with the rich and aristocratic for many generations. I can easily be moved to tears by music or by high works of literature, and although there are those who would consider this to be slushy sentimentality, I believe that the difference in my response is caused by the difference in the situation. In theoretical and practical matters I am required to act, whereas in the contemplation of a work of art I may certainly give reign to my emotions. Goethe shared this predicament. His famous exhortation to be without emotions was scarcely consistent with his personal life. Haldane, who had a highly developed social conscience, and claimed to be both egalitarian and humane, was tyrannical, reckless and capricious in his personal relationships.

The battle today is not so much between good and evil or light and dark, but between Bacchus and Apollo. In the tragedies of Euripides is the most dramatic representation of this conflict, but I cannot help concluding that the playwright is on the side of revolution and chaos. Myself, I prefer Spinoza.

A curious modern phenomenon is a kind of negative hypocrisy. People who privately adhere to the old-fashioned virtues of fidelity, honesty and consideration will nevertheless go to great lengths to defend all sorts of deviations, and argue not only that these should be tolerated, but that they are just as valid as the old patterns of social behaviour. Such people declare that they would fight for the rights of others to hold and express opinions with which they themselves wholeheartedly disagree, and they erroneously cite Voltaire in defence of this position. It is liberalism going mad. Naturally I believe that one should consult other people's opinions, but having thought things through, I believe that one's own views should be staunch and staunchly maintained.

Emotionally a slow developer, I remember being astonished and even slightly disgusted when I noticed the devastating effects of calf-love among my schoolmates. I watched with horror as the most gifted boys in my class fell in love and lost all their intellectual interests. A close friend of mine with a passion for astronomy, geology and physics, was suddenly quite unable to cope, had to be coached by his girlfriend, and almost failed his routine examinations.

Many people, and I include myself, would describe Hans Kalmus as neither particularly sympathetic nor especially soft-hearted but, surprisingly perhaps, students and younger colleagues have often come to me for help, and wept on my shoulder. On several occasions people – and especially women – whom I have only fleetingly met have told me their life histories, their religious attitudes, and all manner of intimate things, without my giving them the slightest hint that I would be particularly suitable or useful, or indeed that I would even welcome their confessions.

Years ago with a colleague of mine, his wife, and their two young daughters I was enjoying an evening stroll after a long and strenuous day at a scientific conference. I can no longer remember what we talked about but I must have made a profound impression on the older of the girls. Many years later I received a letter from her father telling that she was suffering from leukaemia. She had been admitted as a patient to Bart's Hospital where she had been a student nurse, and she had particularly requested that I should visit her. I was astonished but agreed and bought some daffodils and a box of chocolates. Before I entered the ward, the sister told me that my young friend had had a remission and was quite happily talking to her ex-colleagues and was confident about her future. When I saw her, I thought how radiant she looked and she was in very high spirits, chattering away about her plans. But after a few minutes she recited to me the story of another student nurse with leukaemia, who had enjoyed remissions during which she had shown every confidence that she would recover and great hope for the future. Then she told me that the confidence was misplaced and that the girl had been dead for a few months. I did not know what to say. Was she mocking me, or had she persuaded herself that her case was quite different? I left in some confusion. A few months later I heard that she was dead, but had died with a firm belief in salvation and assured that within a few days a mass would be read for her soul.

Emotional or not, I have always loved poetry. At home and at school it was traditional to learn many of the German classics and I can still recite them. The Latin authors did not particularly impress me, but I remember having chanted long passages from the *Iliad* and *Odyssey* while extemporising on the piano, and I know chunks of Homer by heart. Indeed, I enjoy poetry in many languages, though I find contemporary English poetry almost unreadable. Whenever

111

the mood takes me I still compose poetry in German; it clears my moods and clarifies my emotions, and it is good exercise for my creative and critical faculties. Poetry, I believe, has a triple discipline. It must make sense, it must have a coherent form, and it must not only follow a logical pattern but also the rules of aesthetic writing. Clearly, I would not regard much of today's verse as qualifying as poetry.

8

O, Brave New World

My trip to Canada was the precursor of several professional trips abroad, which greatly enhanced my post-war years. In 1954 Dr Elizabeth Goldschmidt, lecturer in genetics at the University of Jerusalem, appeared in my lab and invited me to visit the state of Israel and give some courses in human genetics. Besides a natural curiosity to visit the new country, Nussy's three brothers lived there, and so the offer was extremely welcome. But I pointed out that I had been brought up a Protestant and could not be considered an authentic Jew. Would not that bar me from an official invitation? Apparently not and my trip was sponsored by the Anglo-Hebrew Society which promotes the interests of Jerusalem University. So Nussy and my little daughter Elsa and I set out in the spring, by train to Marseilles, where we enjoyed an excellent bouillabaisse, and by boat to Haifa.

The liner was Italian and was packed with people visiting the Holy Land, Christian pilgrims amidst Jews of every degree of religious orthodoxy. There was one extremely orthodox rabbi, who walked about the decks followed at a distance by his most beautiful wife, who was wearing an ill-fitting wig. The couple made themselves most unpopular because they refused the kosher cooking of the ship's chef and created mysterious dishes in their cabin, the smells of which permeated the corridors. We berthed in Naples and while we were watching Stromboli erupting in the night, I was called to attend an old man who had suffered a heart attack. I spent the night at his bedside and tried to comfort his fears that he might never see the family he had been waiting so many years to see. Happily, he disembarked safely at Haifa the following day.

But there had been other problems *en route*. Rounding Rhodes we struck one of those huge storms which Homer has described so graphically. The furniture and luggage in our cabin were shifting and little Elsa became a little seasick and rather more frightened. Trembling in her bed she asked perhaps whether we all must die? Having passed the cape and sailed into the lee of the wind, the waves abated and within a half-hour she was happily playing on deck. At the quayside at Haifa Dr Goldschmidt and my three brothers-in-law and their wives awaited us. For four weeks Nussy and Elsa were to stay on the dunes of Haifa Bay with two of her brothers, while I lectured in Jerusalem and returned to be with them at weekends.

In 1955, while boarding a steamer in Piraeus, I was handed a telegram from Nussy, congratulating me on being awarded the International Dreyfus Prize for Genetics. This was in the gift of the University of São Paulo and I had quite forgotten that I had been a candidate. Having settled our belongings in a cabin, and with the ship safely at sea, I withdrew the crumpled telegram from my pocket and perused it rather more carefully. The prize money, it seemed, was one million cruzeiros. Not having any idea how much this might be, I concluded that any currency running into millions for a scientific award was unlikely to be worth very much. At that time the cruzeiro did not figure in official currency lists and was not quoted in the newspapers, and it was not until I arrived at Basle railway station that it emerged that my prize was officially valued at some £8,000, although on the unofficial exchange all I could expect to get was about £700. Clearly the sensible thing to do was to spend the money in Brazil, the country of 'unlimited impossibilities', so I obtained leave from my college and travel funds from the Rockefeller Foundation.

It was a complicated trip in those days and I had to travel via Trinidad and Barbados. Flying over Rio de Janeiro Bay, I was chiefly struck by the numerous white elephants of unfinished building projects, notably a huge complex which was intended as a people's hospital but had been sited too far from the *favelas* with their teeming millions to be of any practical use. Professor Cavalcanti, who was to be my host at the Genetical Institute of Rio de Janeiro,

114

met me at the airport. I was welcome to work at the Institute for as long as I felt it profitable to do so.

Most of the work being conducted there was diffuse and ill-directed. The only competent scientist worked on an interesting condition then thought to be hereditary but which in fact was a spirochete infection of *Drosophila*, transmitted through the female – a sort of venereal disease. The doctor, who was of Russian/Jewish descent, was exceedingly helpful to me in my work on some genetical features of the *favela* people, and together we tested their tasting ability and their colour vision, and we even took blood from a considerable number of people living in these shanty towns, a slightly hazardous operation.

The logistics of collecting data of human genetics are complex and diverse. As far as clinical material is concerned, most patients are willing and eager to provide information about their own history and the history of disease in their family. But the problems are more severe when one tries to persuade perfectly healthy people, who cannot derive any benefit from their co-operation, to volunteer tests or information. In a tribe one tries to persuade the head man or some wise old woman to induce their fellow tribesmen and women to take the tests. In more sophisticated societies organisations such as the military or the police are not difficult to recruit once one gets the consent of a high authority. In schools there are often problems. Some years ago there was a letter in *Nature* and a subsequent note in the *Guardian* enquiring whether the method used all over the world for testing the taste threshold of children might not be dangerous. The *Guardian* article was headlined provocatively: 'Are we poisoning our children?' It is perfectly true that young rats given very high dosages of phenylthiocarbonide (PTC) will die, but the smaller dosages given to humans have resulted in no ill effects amongst the tens of thousands, probably even hundreds of thousands, of those so tested. Despite this, school authorities are reluctant to give permission for children to be tested with something that kills rats. Consequently research in Britain has become very difficult, if not impossible.

Thanks to my generous award I led a comfortable life in the country, and spent some interesting days visiting the most beautiful parts of the city and also such watering places as Petropolis and Terrasopolis. I had spent some time in Naples a few months earlier

115

and could compare the two cities. Despite the similarities I had no doubt that Rio is far more magnificent than Naples can ever have been. Climbing up to the monument of Christ on the Hunchback, or by cable car to the Sugar Loaf, watching the blue butterflies in the woods, or bathing under the volcanic chimneys in the bays, were incomparable experiences.

Besides my plan to study the genetical composition of various Indian and modern populations within Brazil, I also intended to study the sun orientation of honey-bees in the southern hemisphere. This research took me to Piracicaba – 'the place where the fish leaps' – an agricultural research station in the state of São Paulo. The leaping fish cataracts still exist and the fish still leap, and plenty of stone arrows may still be found in the neighbouring fields. The director of the research station, Professor Brieger, and the geneticists there were extremely hospitable as I studied the bees, and made possible my forays into the countryside to bleed the local people.

Lindauer and von Frisch had proved that honey-bees possess a kind of astronomical clock which allows them to take into account when navigating the apparent daily movements of the sun. My task in Piracicaba was to discover how the honey-bees compensate in the southern hemisphere when the sun's movement across the sky is anti-clockwise. Bees from stock which had lived locally for many years had adjusted perfectly, but bees which had only recently been transferred from North America behaved as if they were still there. (My results were later challenged, and I myself was at something of a loss as to how to interpret them accurately. I was dependent on the observations of Indian agricultural workers.)

There remain two outstanding problems which have not been attacked. Could not bees from the north be forced to adapt to their new environment much as left-handed people may be made to perform tasks against their natural propensity? The second problem, which has been partially investigated, concerns bees between the Tropics of Cancer and Capricorn, where the sun sometimes moves its azimuth clockwise and sometimes anti-clockwise. It appears that these equatorial bees indulge in a siesta, which I interpret as suggesting that at times of bad orientation they prefer not to go nectar or pollen collecting.

My technique was to train the bees in a sugar-cane field for several days in one direction, then, on the evening of the last training day transport the closed hive by lorry to another sugar-cane field some miles distant. The following morning I would test in which direction the bees were searching for their food. On one such occasion I dropped a hive which broke to the fury of the bees. I was stung by many dozens of them, but to no serious effect.

9

The Little God and the Tower that won't Rust

Nussy and I have been lucky. Modern technology and tropical medicine have enabled us to travel safely and work usefully in places once known as 'white man's graves'. Furthermore, since people are able to enjoy good health longer than in the past we were able to travel in middle age when we may have been less impressionable than when we were younger but were more capable, I believe, of assessing new and changing situations.

The situations were changing most rapidly in Africa, and it was from West Africa, the new University of Ife in Nigeria to be precise, that we were able to observe them. I was invited to teach and examine on several occasions between 1965 and 1974. While British administrators and soldiers were being repatriated, teachers and research workers were welcomed to the newly independent states. I first visited Ife under a scheme by which metropolitan university teachers were temporarily seconded to the new universities in the ex-colonies; my official task was to introduce the teaching of genetics to the Zoology Department.

We travelled on an English liner, manned by an English crew, and we were waited upon by coloured stewards. Most of the first-class passengers were Europeans; there was only a small second class. A few local people travelled between African stops in the steerage. On later journeys all this changed; to begin with the number of Europeans declined and the number of Africans increased; then the boats were bought and run by a Nigerian company; finally, the vast majority of travellers opted to fly, and only bulk cargo was carried by sea.

On a cold, wet December day in 1965 Nussy and I boarded the liner *Accra* of the Elder-Dempster Line for the 13-day trip from Liverpool to Apapa, the harbour of the Nigerian capital, Lagos. Two botanists and a physicist with their families, also bound for Nigerian universities, joined us. A more unusual fellow-traveller was a 14-foot python for which I had undertaken to be responsible. This was not a case of coals to Newcastle for the snake was actually an Indian python whom the reptile keeper of Bristol Zoo had reared, measured and weighed from early youth. Having recently been appointed head keeper of Ibadan Zoo, my colleague had asked me to bring the beast out to him so that he could continue his measurements. Nussy was apprehensive to begin with and declared that where the cabin was concerned I must choose between her and the python, but, as soon as I assured her that the python would travel in a separate animal room, she raised no further objections and indeed was to become friends with the beautiful creature. Having been fed a rabbit shortly before departure, the python required no further nourishment. It was handed to me coiled up in a huge wicker basket, and I was required to visit it each day at noon and pour a can of water over it. I was usually accompanied by half-a-dozen children when it came to 'watering the snake'.

After a rough 24 hours around the Bay of Biscay we reached calmer, warmer seas. The swimming pool was filled, we played deck-tennis and shuffle-board, and shot, hopefully, at clay pigeons. After a short excursion to Las Palmas the journey became a paradise. Shoals of dolphins danced around the boat and from time to time a flying fish landed on the deck. A bright, wonderful moon hung in the sky.

I always arranged on sea journeys for Nussy and me to be seated at the ship's doctor's table. It was a way of ensuring interesting table companions, but on this occasion we were out of luck. We found ourselves landed with a Harley Street specialist, a crotchety old man, snobbish, money-grabbing and reactionary. My daughter, then a medical student, had warned me about such fellows, but this chap was worse than any even she had met. He talked about the varicose veins of his favourite, aristocratic patients. He boasted that he had never employed a woman as a houseman – they were capricious and woke him up at night. He hated negroes and refused to go ashore anywhere in Africa. Most surprisingly he refused to have anything to do with death.

One evening a steward came to our table with the news that an old seaman had collapsed and died. The Harley Street man refused to see him or undertake a post-mortem. Instead he asked me, a passenger, to take a look and confirm his diagnosis of death from a heart attack. The body lay on the floor next to a table on which stood a half-empty glass of beer. Rigor mortis had set in. Several companions had witnessed the man's sudden collapse. The following evening I attended his burial at sea. As a rule deaths on passenger liners are kept secret from the passengers, but, having been involved I asked to be present. The body lay on a lower deck, wrapped in a sack, weighted down with ballast, in the glare of a searchlight. The Captain, attended by as many of the crew as could be spared, read the committal, whereupon a whistle was blown, and the body plunged into the water followed by a wreath. The light was extinguished and the small, silent crowd dispersed into the darkness.

We made our first African landfall on Boxing Day into Freetown, Sierra Leone. Freetown was little changed from colonial days. Hot humid air carrying an indefinable but pungent smell pervaded the decks even before the boat had been secured at the quay. Huge crowds of noisy, garishly-clad locals milled around. Behind the old-fashioned customs house a huge tree grew, in the shadow of which slaves used to be auctioned. Half-way up the hill modern buildings, the university, the governor's modest palace, and the Israeli-built parliament, impinged on our first sight of old Africa. Then we were taken by bus to a beautiful sandy beach where we undressed in a dilapidated clubhouse and had a glorious swim in the warm sea. I loved my first sight of Africa: vultures, weaver birds, butterflies; oil palms, bougainvillaea, hibiscus, frangipani; the grey English winter seemed far away, and so did such dreary matters as theories and significance tests. My juvenile obsession with absorbing facts had come into its own again.

Our next port of call was Accra. We drove past an impressive statue of Nkrumah – it had been removed by the time we revisited the place. An enormous 'black' square, in imitation of Moscow's Red Square, was completely deserted, but the streets and markets were thronged with people. When we returned to the boat and the cool air-conditioning, we watched as local boys dived into Accra harbour for pennies thrown by the passengers.

Ile Ife, the holy town in the centre of Yorubaland, was chosen as the site for the regional university and construction had just started when Nussy and I first visited it. (Up until then the university had been in Ibadan.) We arrived by Landrover and picnicked in front of the first building to be built; it was then about half completed. Its long axis had been planned to run east to west so that the sun would never be directly opposite the principal façade, and the higher storeys overhung the lower ones to shade them from the vertical midday sun. A few access roads had been bulldozed in the bush, but otherwise the campus – 13,500 acres of it – was undisturbed. It encompassed sizeable hills, brooks, villages, swamps and meadows, but principally woods. When I was last there some 10 years ago several thousand undergraduates were swarming between huge institutes, dormitories and sports areas.

The students were equally divided between the sexes. Most were Yorubas; there were some Nigerians from other tribes, and a very few British and American students. Of the Nigerian first-year students, half needed remedial English classes. These were conducted, quite competently, by a Greek lady. The majority of the students attending my classes had illiterate and often polygamous parents. Although they were nominally Christian, the secular European culture which engulfed them must have seemed very strange. They were only insecurely anchored in the university ambience, and prone to relapse into the habits and perspectives of their tribal African childhoods. The mixture of the magical and the scientific produced bizarre conflicts in their young souls.

For some reason the Yoruba people have the highest twinning rate in the world. My steward had two pairs of twins and was a twin himself. The question as to whether twins are monozygotic or dizygotic, that is, whether they are the products of one or two fertilised eggs, is an intriguing one and to study it properly one needs to know the various properties of the placenta. An investigation into just this topic was going on at the Galton Laboratory at the time of my Nigerian visit, so I arranged the speedy transportation of twin placentae from Ibadan to London Airport.

The Registrar of the University, an elderly and somewhat Anglicised Sinhalese, and a strict disciplinarian, was unpopular

121

with the radical students, and his job was coveted by a local man. Several attempts to have him replaced had failed and finally magic was tried. One morning the Registrar showed me a cloth doll, into which several large pins had been stuck and which he had found on his desk. He understood the message though he did not heed it.

On another occasion it was I who found myself confronted with superstitions and superstitious fears. Nussy had promised a colleague to collect palm prints of 100 male and 100 female Yorubas. So I asked my class to come forward and have their prints taken. This immediately aroused suspicion because the method, involving printer's ink, was the same as that used by the police, and some of the boys who had been involved in demonstrations concluded that I must be a police agent. No sooner had I settled these fears than I was accused of racialism, because I only wanted prints of Yoruba palms. I at once agreed to take skin ridges from anybody, though the prints of the non-Yorubas would be useless, and Nussy was required to ink, print and wash several dozen additional sweaty hands. More deep-seated was the fear, never expressed, that to have a likeness taken, whether a photograph or a palm print, was to lose a part of one's personality. I could not at first understand why so few of my usually friendly and eager first-year students came to be palm printed. In the end I had to turn to the third-year medics and even then I had to impress on them that they might care to do something for me who had, after all, come all the way to Nigeria to teach them. It had been fruitless trying to explain to them why palm and finger prints were of anthropological interest.

The tables were turned when I was asked to participate in the Nigerian census, a highly controversial event. A week or so before the day of the count we were visited by a local teacher, the census officer for our part of the campus, accompanied by a soldier armed with both pistol and rifle. The objections to the census were not those one might have expected in Europe, were not to do with bureaucratic interference or taxes, but again related to genuine concerns about the loss of personality. Hence the heavily armed guard. On census day itself the same couple arrived with a huge bundle of forms. The questions were well phrased but grotesque. After the usual requests for date and place of birth, religion and so on, I was asked my profession. I answered: 'University professor.' The next question staggered me. 'Could I read or write?' Then I was asked what languages other than my native Nigerian I could speak. I said English, German, French and some Italian, but I was interrupted to be told that French and German were actually the same language. Later I realised that if I had been asked the difference between the two major Nigerian languages I would have been equally at a loss.

There was another occasion which might have been dangerous. With a few young colleagues and students I had climbed a sizeable inselberg, one of those granite outcrops which rise sheer from the plains of Africa. As was common in such cases, the village on the top of the plateau had been deserted during the Pax Britannica as the inhabitants had felt safe to move nearer to their fields. But they had left their gods behind, and I was told that there was a small idol hidden in a cave half-way down the steep east wall, which on certain nights was brought out and worshipped. I demanded to be led to the cave, and when I took the little god out into the sun to photograph it, some of my friends expected me to be struck down by thunder, much like St Boniface, when he felled the oak tree. I was also told that one or two of the students had felt inclined to make themselves the instrument of the god's wrath. But I returned him to his holy cave and for all that I know he is still there and still being worshipped from time to time.

During an excursion, on which we were accompanied by some American colleagues, Nussy and I had a strange experience for which to this day we have no explanation. One Sunday morning on the way to a remote valley, where the worship of dogs had persisted, we passed through a half-mile-long village, full of boutiques displaying plastic buckets and household articles, local food and dresses and many other saleables. The road was thronged with happy, noisy people, and our car could progress only slowly. At the end of the settlement the crowd thinned and we noticed a string of young men and women moving slowly in single file out of the village. At the head of the procession, as if in a trance, walked a huge, white-haired, black woman, stark naked. Whenever the woman stopped, those behind her stopped also. As the procession continued we observed that the young men and women, whose movements had become dance-like, were watching the old woman intently and proceeding in complete silence. After a short discussion we left this disturbing scene behind and continued to our destination where we found the skulls of many dogs embedded in the walls of a village of mud huts.

We returned by a different route and were amused by the excitement of a group of small boys. They had not, we concluded, seen white faces before and ran beside our car shouting the news at the top of their voices. I was told that they were calling us 'the peeled ones', meaning that originally we must have been dark like everybody else, but that our dark skins must have been peeled off. Back on our old route but some distance along the road from where we had seen the morning's procession, Nussy spotted a huge, dark mass lying in a ditch. At first we took this for a dead cow, but it was not. It was the naked old woman, and, when we stopped to look more closely, we discovered that she was dead. The body was already stiff; there were no signs of violence upon it. We deliberated as to whether or not we ought to call the police, but our American friends warned us against it; it was dangerous, they said, to get involved in other people's deaths.

We never found out how or why the old lady had died. An anthropologist suggested that we might have witnessed the expulsion of a witch; a priest thought that it might have been a purifying act of self-sacrifice.

Unlike other countries of the Third World, West African countries in general, and Nigeria in particular, have not yet become tourist playgrounds. Airlines and navigable roads, and fundamental social changes accelerated by the country's oil wealth have led to a transformation interesting to the sociologist, the biologist and, indeed, to any concerned person.

On the one hand there is the 'old' Africa, primitive villages and beaches, mangrove and rain forests, savannah and deserts, each studded with individual flora and fauna. On the other hand harbours, industrial developments, prosperous universities and urban slums represent the new world. Additionally, there are the vast projects such as the dam construction at Kainji, which produced, in addition to electricity, an 80-mile-long lake in the middle course of the Niger. Around a reserve adjoining Kainji one could find elephants, lions and several species of antelope, all this in an area previously almost devoid of large animals. And everywhere quantities of diverse people trying to become 'modern' with all the stresses that entails. It amounts to an enormous experiment in social change as fascinating – and sometimes as uncomfortable – as may be found anywhere.

A striking example of these profound changes is that the most significant cause of premature death has changed from epidemic infectious diseases to road accidents. In Ife University there was some cholera, but nobody died from it. Within a few months I was aware of four separate fatal road accidents on the campus roads, and the road from Lagos to the coast was littered with the decomposing wrecks of cars and lorries.

I am not convinced that my intention to start a Department of Genetics at Ife and train a nucleus of research workers there to carry on was especially successful. One of my American colleagues, a Professor of American History, put it rather more cynically when he remarked that his only achievement at Ife was to teach the dozens of children of his black colleagues to swim. I do, however, believe that I helped all sorts of unexpected projects in all sorts of unexpected ways, and that the months I spent in Nigeria were amongst the most rewarding and fruitful of my life.

Many years ago an old colleague remarked to me: 'Who has not seen India has not seen life.' At that time I thought the remark extravagant, but I came to appreciate what he meant, and what I had missed by not setting foot in India until I was 70.

My first contact with India was quite bizarre. My mother took me, at the age of 12, to a recital by Rabindranath Tagore. It was certainly wasted on me, being delivered in an incomprehensible language, whether in English or in an Indian dialect I cannot remember. But what I shall always remember is the tall and venerable figure of the great man. I think that it also helped me to appreciate that somewhere there existed a civilisation quite apart from my own.

Many years after this, when in Heligoland, breeding oysters for the Prussian government, I fell into conversation with an Indian fishery expert. As we walked that night and for several subsequent nights along the red cliffs, I was the recipient of his fervent enthusiasm for Indian freedom, and his striking ambivalence towards England, a characteristic of many Indians. He spoke of brutal oppression by the occupying force. I asked him how many Britons were employed in oppressing how many Indians. Being an honest man he confessed that between 50,000 and 100,000 British were living amongst many hundred millions of Indians. When I invited him to explain how so many people could possibly be brutally kept down by so few he was rather taken aback and we abandoned the subject. He was also ambivalent towards British institutions. When I asked him why, bearing in mind his hatred of England, he had enrolled as a student at Cambridge rather than at Heidelberg or Paris, he said plainly that he did so because 'Cambridge was best'.

My next Indian encounter many years later in Prague was an audience with Pandit Nehru. It was shortly before the Munich crisis and Nehru, recently released from prison, was touring Europe, talking to anti-Hitler politicians and trying to understand the nature of the madness. I had concluded by then that my scientific future lay elsewhere than in Central Europe and my parents pulled strings through their university connections to arrange for me to have an audience with the Indian leader. I was received in his room in the Hotel Alcron, and he listened patiently to my enquiry, in inadequate English, as to the possibilities of researching in India. A young, bright-eyed woman, whom I took to be his wife, was also present. I realised later that she was his daughter, Mrs Gandhi, the future Prime Minister of India. The Pandit did not think much of my plans to work in his country. He had been persuaded by President Benes, and other confident politicians, that the dangers I had perceived were illusory, and he assured me that my place was in Prague where I would happily live, work and die in a democratic Czechoslovakia. I took my leave, unsure whether to laugh or cry.

In London my Indian connections had continued. I vividly recall my first Indian restaurant, to which I was invited by Dr. N. K. Pannikkar, a postgraduate student in zoology and later to become the head of Indian Fisheries. I thought I was being offered fire to eat and became extremely hot and bothered to my colleague's great amusement. In India and in Mexico I was to become familiar with, and fond of, highly spiced food.

In Harpenden one of my colleagues was Mr (later Dr) Bamji, a Parsee, about whom I have written in Chapter 5. He was a fervent Communist and described to anyone who would listen the terrible conditions in the slums of Bombay and Calcutta. His most telling statistics related to the number of lavatories per person per tenement.

Haldane's association with Indian biology and statistics brought him into contact with several Indians, but he was jealously concerned to keep me away from the famous Mahanalobis, the chief of the

Calcutta Statistical Institute, when he visited the department. Most of my Indian acquaintances were PhD students of Imperial College, whom I met as their external examiner. In principle, the standards applied to these students should have been as high as for the British students; in practice this was neither possible nor fair. In any case the internal examiner would have already supervised the theses and passed them, so what I was in effect called upon to do was to pronounce on this colleague. If I were critical I would antagonise senior colleagues and discourage younger ones. Inevitably I made some enemies, but not, I think, amongst the Indian students. In due course after Professor Gruneberg had encouraged me to travel to India, I was cordially and hospitably received by many of them and by the universities and institutions in which they had found employment.

We arrived early one November morning at New Delhi Airport, where we were met by Dr Manjit S. Grevall, a tall, bearded Sikh, working at the Indian Medical Research Institute. After a comprehensive tour of the capital he set off for his home, and we noticed candles in the windows of many houses and flowers laid out in elaborate patterns by the doors of the houses. It was Divali, the festival of light, and the most propitious day we could have chosen to arrive in India. Grevall's French wife gave us a delicious dinner, Indian cooking softened by a Provençal influence, and I drank a lot of beer. The meal over, we went up on to the flat roof and watched the fireworks, to the intense excitement of the Grevall's turbaned young son.

Our next weeks we spent sightseeing in Delhi, Agra and Gwalior, travelling by plane, train and rickshaw, staying in hotels and palaces and trying to absorb the rich extravagance of everything to which we were being exposed. There was friendliness on all sides, no hint of Anglophobia. Often we found it difficult to turn down the hospitality being offered to us by complete strangers. The research being done in the medical institutions was less impressive.

It would be foolish of me to attempt a serious consideration of India after two months' travel in the country, but some observations which I noted down in my diary (and which Nussy noted down in hers) still seem intriguing.

I discovered that, unlike the Egyptians and Chinese, the Indians have never been especially interested in their history. Detailed historiography was until recently only pursued by British scholars, and, since these men could only draw on scanty and diffused records, long periods of regional history remain hazy. My colleague C. J. Rao, the biometrician, succeeded in establishing a fifteenth-century dynasty of local kings by an archaeological method. He studied the coins of the period. The oldest had lost most weight through excessive handling. Since the coins all bore the kings' effigies he was able to determine the sequence of the rulers through their comparative weights.

The lack of so much history may have contributed to a striking uncertainty about their aims and values which I found amongst many thoughtful, educated Indians. The vastness of the sub-continent and the fragmentation of its people through language, religion and caste have also made it difficult for a clearly defined *Indian* personality to emerge. The Indians we spoke to set most store by their regional alliances. They regarded themselves as Punjabis, Bengalis, Rajasthans, or Tamils first, and Indians a long way second.

It seems to me that the strongest factor for the emergence of a unified and identifiable India has been the British. They have made positive contributions, a lingua franca and an infrastructure. And by their presence and domination they have unified the forces of resentment and resistance. The modern Indians whom we encountered were the children of parents who had defeated the Raj, but they had willingly embraced Western values. Indian democracy owes as much to Bloomsbury as to Gandhi.

India's contribution to the sciences has been most noticeable in astronomy, mathematics and physics. We visited the two surviving Yantras, stone observatories, five of which had been built by Jai Singh, the Moghul king, warrior and savant between 1718 and 1743. These vast structures, one in Delhi, the other in Jaipur, reminded me of the famous Oranienburg, Tycho Brahe's observatory on the Swedish island of Ven. Before sophisticated telescopes were invented these observatories provided astronomers with the best means for accurate star-gazing. In Jaipur I was impressed particularly with the Samrat Tower, a 70-foot-high gnomon, the shadow of which was used to time noon, the equinoxes, etc. Here the midday sun is sometimes to the north, sometimes to the south, so that two huge, hollow scales had had to be built adjacent to the tower. It was a vivid demonstration of two aspects of time to watch while the edge of the tower's shadow inexorably progressed from line to line across the glistening polished stone, as it has done for more than two-and-a-half centuries. Other structures had been designed to trace the movements of the moon and the planets, and there were a dozen 'houses' for the sun, representing the constellations of the Zodiac.

It seems only logical that the sophisticated building techniques of the Indians should have been put to the service of astronomy. But more mysterious is the purpose of the iron pillar, with its Sanskrit inscriptions, which stands adjacent to the huge Moghul tower of Qut Minar and which has been standing there throughout 1,500 monsoon seasons, quite unaffected by rust. We do not know who built this pillar; whoever it was must have been experienced in metallurgy.

Indian zoology and medicine have been impeded by the Hindu belief in reincarnation, the divinity of some animals, and the sanctity of life. In many villages rats are not killed but put into a neighbour's yard. Flies are not swatted, corpses are burnt, and the Brahmins, the educated class, are disdainful of any kind of practical work. One should not wonder, in the circumstances, that nobody undertakes dissection or animal experiments. But the traveller in India cannot fail to notice the special relationship that exists between animals and man. The close association between elephant and mahout, between snake and snake-charmer, the freedom of the cows which are allowed to roam the towns, the jungle monkeys: these are matters which would surely repay scientific investigation. Nussy and I were shown white (albinotic) elephants and rhino in Delhi Zoo. We enjoyed the crowds of storks and pelicans clustering around the ponds, as well as the nature reserves with their wild elephants, crocodiles and jungle fowl. We stayed at the Zoological Institute in Trivandrum and saw a newly-born muntjak foal, tiny but already upright and staggering on its shaky legs. We also saw what every tourist sees, the vultures hovering in the air or fighting over a delicious carcase in a field, the flocks of green parrots flying in the morning beneath the hotel windows in Agra, the wild peacocks on the hills near Gaitor.

Indian botany has its roots in herbalism and one of my most interesting afternoons was spent at the Faculty of Indigenous Medicine which is part of the Hindu University in Varanassi (Benares). Here I was shown experiments to isolate by modern chemical techniques the active 'principles' of traditional folk cures, mainly herbal. When I was there the hibiscus flower was being studied.

Also at Benares was a separate faculty for Western medicine, and the science and arts departments that one finds in European and American universities. But here the boys and girls lived on separate campuses and were forbidden to visit one another. Moreover, although the girls could attend the 'male' lectures, parallel lectures were held where they would avoid being in the presence of boys.

Life is not easy for these students. The resources of most parents are stretched and grants are minimal and hard to come by. How did some of them manage to keep alive? I recall a young postgraduate who received no grant and whose peasant parents were so old that he was obliged several times a year to travel hundreds of miles by bus to help them gather the harvest. He could scarcely afford the fare, yet he seemed well-nourished and was cheerful. I wondered whether the extended family was at work.

There are maybe a dozen well-endowed institutes of higher education and research, maintained by the central government, but the hundreds of state universities and colleges are stunted by poverty. Sometimes the income of a department head was less than the dole in Britain. A subscription to a British or American scientific journal may exceed a half-year's salary for a lecturer; a textbook may cost the equivalent of a professor's monthly income.

The Statistical Institute in Calcutta is centrally funded and world famous. It occupies a vast garden area, surrounded by many square miles of shanty town. Numerous laboratories and accommodation units have been built around the home of the poet and philosopher, Rabindranath Tagore. Mahanalobis, the eminent mathematician, was principally responsible for the place, and its main fields of research are statistics and demography, though in recent years it has branched out into such areas as palaeontology and physiology.

I gave two lectures there on the genetical differences of sensory perception, such as colour-blindness, tune deafness, tasting differences and so on. Amongst my audience I was delighted to spot Professor Pradesh, who had for many years investigated such traits in Indian populations, using my methods. He had left his place of retirement and travelled hundreds of miles to meet me in person for the first time.

The Statistical Institute has developed a special way of commemorating its history. Eminent statesmen and scientists who visit it are invited to plant trees, to which names and dates are attached. As I walked along the avenue of trees of increasing size and majesty, I noticed that some flourished, while others looked rather miserable, and I wondered whether there might be a correlation between the well-being of the tree and the validity in India of the ideas of those who had planted them.

I worry about the future and the role of Western science in India. Modern technology will affect the lives of the inhabitants increasingly of course, but – excepting mathematics and philosophy – penetrating analysis and attempts at synthesis seem unlikely to flourish. Theoretical subjects are alien plants in Indian fields, and British dominance and reverence for British scientists have not yet been challenged.

We visited the University in Hyderabad, where we hoped to see Helen Spurway, Haldane's widow, and we were lucky enough to see her, because shortly after our visit she died from tetanus. As we emerged from the plane we heard her shrill voice in the distance, and, as we approached the customs building, we saw her haranguing several groups of men excitedly. It transpired that these were the various delegations for the Vice Chancellor, who had arrived on the same aircraft as us, and for ourselves. We were given the traditional welcoming garlands, but there was some dispute as to whether we were to stay in the guest-house of the University or in a hotel in the town. In the end we were whisked away to Helen's ramshackle large house, where we stayed for a couple of days, before being abducted by the wife of the Vice-Chancellor.

Helen's house was part museum and part menagerie. On the ground floor was Haldane's extensive library, growing mouldy and being nibbled at by rats. On the first floor we shared a room with a more-or-less tame jackal, two mongrel dogs, several cats, mynah birds, jungle fowl, tortoises and three colonies of wasps, which were nesting on the ceiling above our bed. Helen was accumulating notes on the behaviour of all these creatures. I really admired Nussy, who is not a trained zoologist, but who never batted an eye at the squalid disorder. On our second evening there the Vice-Chancellor and his family, the Dean and other colleagues came to tea, which was served by Helen's cook on the tables used occasionally

131

for dissections and other anatomical experiments. When I expressed some bewilderment at the bizarre goings-on, it was explained to me that Indian scientists owed a great debt of gratitude to Haldane, who had devoted the last years of his life to the sub-continent, and who, together with Helen, acquired Indian citizenship. The awe felt towards the Haldanes became apparent to me when I lectured. On several occasions, when I was introduced to the audience, special reference was made to the distinguished presence in the hall of 'Dr Helen Spurway-Haldane'. Haldane's achievements were of course well known, but I doubt whether anybody there knew what Helen's contribution to biology had been.

In those countries in which I have observed the clash of Western civilisation on primitive peoples, I was confronted with two possible responses. One could deal with the problem as those who believed themselves to be well-intentioned dealt with the North American Indians and the New Zealand Maoris. After periods of the most inhumane treatment, reserves were created in which the indigenous people could maintain their life-style, as though the white man had never arrived in their midst. To me such enclaves are undignified. People contained within them who are not enjoying full citizens' rights are more akin to animals in the zoo than to members of our own species. Nor do they flourish, physically, spiritually or culturally. Their songs and dances degenerate into a sort of show business, their pottery and artefacts are vulgarised for the tourist trade, their lives lose all tribal importance.

The alternative is assimilation, which also leads inevitably to demoralisation and all sorts of social problems. I can offer no satisfactory solution to this. All that can be done is to try and make the transition period a little less disastrous, and to rescue and preserve those few elements which have a value for the larger society. I will not believe that this kind of assimilation necessarily leads to a drab, uniform kind of humanity.

Although I have never had a very strong capacity or inclination to form close relationships, I have not found it difficult to strike up *ad hoc* friendships with people from other cultures. The politeness in Latin countries can have rather ridiculous consequences. In Brazil I was once assured by a man whom I had met only five minutes before that his house, all his possessions, his car and his time were entirely at my disposal. I was sorely tempted to ask whether this generosity also included his wife. Contrastingly, the interest and sympathy of Indians I have casually met at a park bench or visiting a temple or staying at a hotel are genuine and touching. My students in Africa and the tribal people in Amazonia with whom I had dealings were at first cautious, suspicious and reticent. But sometimes I found that I could overcome this resistance. In the case of my students, enthusiasm for their ideas helped me to win them over. With the tribal people, being a doctor and helping them to overcome disease within their families quickly broke the ice. As far as I can remember I am still Honorary President of a football club on the Brazilian-Argentinian border, simply because in a town 20 miles away I gave them some money to buy a football. They sent a runner overnight to collect it.

10

The Pleasures of Playfulness

I retired from my chair at University College on 30 September 1973, at the end of the academic year in which I had reached the age of 67 years. At the end of the summer term my colleagues had arranged for me the customary farewell dinner with speeches and a presentation – a set of suitcases to take on my imminent trip to Nigeria. One of my nieces, a student at the College, gave me a fountain pen, and Nussy some roses. There was a conversazione at the Royal Society that evening, but, despite this, many eminent people came, some doggerel was produced, and I was given a drawing captioned with a quotation from Pliny the Elder: 'ex Africa semper aliquid novi'.

Retirement did not change my life greatly. My income scarcely decreased, although I missed the research budget and the secretarial help I had been accustomed to at the College. In West Germany, Brazil and many other states, a professor retains not only his full salary after retirement, but may also claim a room, some space in the laboratory and staff to help with research; no such obligations exist in British universities. I am able, however, to do a certain amount of experimental work in the department, and, thanks to the generosity of the College, I may still use the library and a small cubby-hole of my own. Once a year I continued to give a lecture and a practical, usually on the hereditary anomalies of sense perception, for example, colour blindness, tune deafness, or taste deficiency. I had never headed the department, and this, I believe, made the transition smoother. I continued on the sidelines much as before.

I had, of course, gained my freedom. What I could still achieve was dependent on myself and not on external pressures. A sobering thought and a precarious situation. I could come and go as I wanted. But in effect this was no gain, because it removed the framework of my working week, and replaced it with additional chores, such as the writing of this autobiography.

In retirement I travelled even more extensively and I found, with Goethe, that 'human life, wherever I touched it, was full of interest'. My file remained full of projects in various stages of elaboration. All my life I have taken on too much, running too many experiments simultaneously writing them up in two or three languages. But I have probably not achieved much less than if I had been more single-minded; except, perhaps, recognition. While I have had no difficulty in renouncing many things, drug-taking and sexual excess for instance, I could never restrain my powerful creative instincts.

I sometimes wonder what would have become of me if I had been born rich. I might well have become a playboy. But my family's modest circumstances and puritanical instincts ensured that luxury and ostentation made little appeal. My wife and I live a very simple life and, when she is away from home, I soon relapse into the habits of an impecunious student.

But there have been times when I have sampled the high life, and found them pleasant enough to be memorable. Once the International Atomic Energy Commission appointed me consultant to the President of Mexico and furnished me with a diplomatic passport. Landing in New York after sampling the food and wine provided by Air France's First Class service, I quite enjoyed the bureaucratic confusion – for I had once carried the passport of a stateless refugee and prohibited immigrant – and later in Mexico City the police escort, the trappings of eminence, the press interviews and the cameras. We were met by Dr Alfonso Leon de Garay, the father of human genetics in Mexico, and now an ambassador of his country, and as we drove into the town, we found it beflagged and illuminated and thronged with animated crowds. The huge Zocalo (main square) with the cathedral and the governor's palace was a grandiose sight. But I was not too surprised to learn that the city was in the process of welcoming the President of the United States as well as Nussy and me! But there were still receptions and banquets in our honour, and the ceremonial planting of a tree, which Nussy much appreciated.

It was while I was on a previous assignment in Mexico City that my host arranged for my portrait to be painted by Raoul Anguiano, famous for his murals in the Museum of Anthropology. I sat for 12 sessions, and was stimulated by the visitors to the atelier. There was the French cultural attaché, old Indians with psychotonic drugs derived from hallucinatory mushrooms, dealers in fake antiques which they claimed to have just dug out of the ground, and pretty nude models, and all the while I had to sit quite still and not say a word. I call Anguiano's picture my Mexican landscape and, although I do not particularly admire it, there are many who do.

Once, at the venerable Dutch University of Leyden, a doctorate was conferred on a young lady who had used some of my methods for investigating colour blindness, and I was required to 'attack' her thesis in the manner of a medieval disputation. The university functionaries were dressed like Rembrandt figures and I was pressed into some academic gown to which I surely had no title. It was an evening of pure theatre, the academic merits or demerits of the thesis having already been widely aired.

On another occasion I found myself in a small group lunching at the House of Lords; our host was a Labour peer, who made several remarks indicating that he was quite jealous of the privileges he enjoyed as a member of the Upper House, and not at all happy about the encroaching arrogance of the Commoners. I left early because I had to attend a meeting of the Board of Studies for Genetics at the Senate House. At the exit of Westminster Palace a burly concierge summoned a taxi for me and, as I climbed in, I could not help realising that in some small but significant way I had become part of the British establishment. I know I felt some satisfaction, but chiefly I remember feeling amazed and amused, as I contemplated my early life.

I have broadcast only rarely and scarcely ever appeared on television, in part because my accent was objected to. But I do not believe that these media are suitable for presenting current research or serious discussion. If ever I felt a little envious of colleagues who were led into the limelight, I observed how they were transformed, even sometimes corrupted. Some ceased to be original researchers or critical thinkers and became performers, actors, 'personalities'.

I am convinced that in order to think scientifically it is essential to resist accepting the unsupported opinions of others, a familiar form of intellectual corruption. In practical everyday situations it follows that a scientist should hesitate to adopt wholesale the attitudes and responses of others. I could never fight other people's ideological battles. In any event human conflicts are traditionally between groups not ideologies. Being a member of a particular ethnic, linguistic or religious group must condition one's attitudes, and give rise to powerful loyalties, but should never cloud one's considered judgement. Whenever possible I believe that I have followed my own intellectual ideas and looked after my own personal affairs. The old Greeks would have described me as an *idiotes*, a private man.

Anyone objectively reviewing my career would conclude that I have been, like Autolycus, 'a snapper-up of unconsidered trifles', and been swayed by the currents and counter-currents that flowed around me, but that impression is partial and incomplete. Episodic and discontinuous beginnings were followed by longer periods of consolidation and modification. I would inquire into apparently unconnected areas of specialisation, and emerge with a coherent pattern; or could it be that the coherence which I later charted was merely a restrospective delusion?

My intention was always to be and remain expert in a very few limited areas, but to be interested in anything which came my way. As Goethe put it: 'Delve into the plenitude of life and find interest in anything you touch.' Haldane always maintained that one should strive to be the best expert in the world on one or two subjects, howsoever tiny they might be. A wide range of knowledge is essential for those inter-disciplinary jumps, which blinkered specialists are incapable of making. A successful transfer of a conceptual system, developed for a particular material, to another formerly unrelated material, that which Koestler called bisociation, can only occur when people have considerable knowledge in different fields. One-discipline specialists may win Nobel prizes, but new disciplines only emerge from versatile minds.

The distinction between the polymath, or universalist, and the specialist has an ethical dimension. It can be argued that the polymath is more egocentric, egoistical, concerned with getting as much insight and enjoyment from the contemplation of as many facets of the world as possible, whereas the specialist more modestly ploughs a narrower field, which may be of considerable and tangible benefit to his fellow men. I prefer a combination of the two.

The time it took me to finish a piece of work varied enormously.

Three weeks was all that was necessary to disentangle earlier research on the mineral requirements of *Drosophila* and to produce a workable formula. But it took 30 years of intermittent work to realise a paper on tune deafness.

Sometimes political events intervened. Experiments on the circadian eclosion of *Drosophila* were interrupted when I was expelled from the laboratory in Prague in the autumn of 1938. When some months later I was again up and running with this line of research the evacuation of my department from London stopped it – for ever, as far as I was concerned. (Others – and most successfully Pittendrigh – later built on my foundations.) Before leaving Prague I had refused to publish in the *gleichgeschalteten*, German journals, which would probably have refused to publish me in any case, and as a result I had to turn to obscure Italian and Austrian periodicals. Then came the war, and the ensuing chaos ensured that my papers would not be read for a further 10 years.

The academic history of Prague has been severely impeded by political events, by interference from the Czech authorities, by the Nazis, who suspended the activities of our German University, and by the Russians, who abolished it. Later academics had to suffer the Communist purges, so that the tradition was constantly interrupted, and standards suffered. I do not believe that political changes should regulate what happens in places of learning and research. The late Dr Adenauer was attacked by many for his failure to de-Nazify the top thinkers in the universities. In my view he was right. It was quite wrong not to remove National Socialists from the judiciary or high administrative officers from the government, but to remove a surgeon or a technician because he or she had been a Nazi, which the majority of people were forced to be, would have greatly hampered the country's recovery. Science and culture have flourished under all sorts of regimes; they are not a monopoly of democracies.

I could not always blame external events for my own shortcomings. Sometimes there would be technical problems, which I could not surmount with the available technology; and sometimes I would get bored with routine work in awkward conditions, and would be seduced by other more immediately interesting work. Occasionally the results of a new experiment would provoke me into compulsive intellectual bouts, jotting down ideas throughout the night. I did not enjoy these episodic explosions, but could not prevent them. Ironically I always felt – and still feel – 'deserted' when they have not occurred for several months.

These manic nights were not limited to scientific matters. Sometimes they would produce poetry; sometimes they would codify masses of accumulated material, experimental, formal or literary. In the grey light of morning I would look at what I had achieved with some disappointment. I learned to leave my notes for a few days and then look at them critically, as though they had been written by somebody else. Then I was often astonished by what I had achieved. But there is no doubt that my energies were dissipated in too many directions, and that more and more of my work would lie unfinished in steel cabinets.

I never lacked starting points for further research; I was never short of material for occasional lectures and reviews. In this way I acquired the reputation of an old-fashioned polymath. To the geneticists I was a sense physiologist; to the ethologists I was a mathematician; to the scientists a doctor; and – inevitably, I suppose – vice versa. A consequence was that referees for my papers frequently failed to understand them. Commenting on my paper on 'Optometer Reactions', which deals with them being controlled by 'quasivectors', one commentator, a zoologist, wrote that it was all incomprehensible, a second, presumably an applied mathematician, that it was all familiar stuff, while a third contented himself with pointing out typing errors. Subsequently this same paper, which I consider my most original, was further rejected by two British journals – again by the above-mentioned zoologist, who finally wrote to me recommending that I try placing it abroad. The typescript was lost in a boat torpedoed on its way to America; a copy sent to Holland was mislaid by its German referee. The delay lasted four years, but it mattered little, for it was hardly noticed until recently. After 40 years it came up in a discussion session, in which I took part, at the Royal Society.

It seems to me that papers breaking new ground encountered great resistance, while humdrum specialist results were published without difficulty. When I worked within my recognised field, my conclusions were more acceptable than when I branched out. At the age of 80 I tried to find a publisher for my first slim volume of German poetry. After a dozen refusals I printed it myself. It was highly praised and well reviewed by the experts; it was greatly appreciated by friends; so far it has reached fewer than 200 people.

I contrast this with my best-selling book *Genetics*, sold in hundreds of thousands by Penguin. I have to accept the view of younger geneticists, impelled to their careers by reading it, that it is a successful book, but I am convinced that its success is in part due to the timing of its publication at the height of the Lysenko controversy. My resulting celebrity demonstrated to me vividly that there is not a high correlation between the effort I put into a piece of work and its success. *Genetics* was dictated during long hours of firewatching, without access to books, just as it came into my head.

Work may fail as a result of being premature, too advanced for its time, or postmature, that is, it could have been achieved earlier. Paradoxically some work may be considered as premature *and* postmature, as I argued in my study of Mendel's famous paper of 1865, which formed the basis of modern genetics.

Another paper, which I value highly, was also rejected by the Royal Society and has never seen the light of day. It is a mathematical theory of the way the brain computes colours in various illuminations and colour backgrounds, a development of Land's work. It is natural to feel some bitterness about these and similar disappointments; it is some small consolation that even Darwin was a victim of similar indifference.

More cheerful are those occasions when the scientist actually sees his teaching being used by others in their research or practical work. Once in a *Drosophila* laboratory I discovered a great many cultures labelled: 'Kalmus I' and 'Kalmus 2'. Enquiries confirmed that my mineral requirement medium was being used extensively in that laboratory. On another occasion I was passing through a classroom in the zoological department of the University of Wisconsin, and I saw on the blackboard some of my bee experiments described. I don't believe there are more gratifying moments in a scientist's life.

Many consider the Royal Society to be a most important institution, and believe that to become a Fellow is one of the greatest honours to which any scholar can aspire. Bertrand Russell's brother believed an FRS to be superior to anyone else on earth, archbishops and prime ministers included, and expressed this view in a letter, dated 3 March 1908, to his celebrated brother. Haldane, despite his iconoclastic tendencies, took a similar position. Of course I am aware that I may be accused of sour grapes, but I am convinced that the Royal Society in its present form is an anachronism. There are so many excellent scientists in the world that it seems invidious to select but a few and to confer on them quite disproportionate powers in making decisions affecting the funding of specialist research. What I believe the Royal Society does usefully provide is a link between the scientific world and the higher echelons of politics and administration.

Early this year (1988) I was very pleased to learn that Peter was awarded the Institute of Physic's Rutherford Medal and Prize 'for outstanding contributions to the discovery of the W and Z particles'. When a few weeks later an old Rothamsted friend – now retired to the West Country – rang me to congratulate me on my son's success, saying: 'I wanted to be the first', I thanked him but said that he was not the first. He was surprised and added: 'But it will not be made public until tomorrow.' After some confusion it turned out that he, as a Fellow of the Royal Society, learnt a day earlier than the official announcement that my younger son, George, had been made a Fellow. This was delightful news indeed and a great satisfaction to me.

I recall a conversation during which I casually mentioned to a friend that I was a lonely person, an individualist who did not easily fit into groups or join associations. At this my wife started to laugh and asked me to count the societies and groups I belonged to. I reached 17 without any difficulty. But in only a few cases have I played a leading role in any of them.

For five years I was President of the Animal Behaviour Society. In my student days I had read Konrad Lorenz's famous study on the behaviour of jackdaws towards their fellows, and it had made a deep impression on me. I had always known thereafter that animals were extremely complicated creatures. So, for instance, I described the change of reactivity of the larvae of stick insects when they crawl up a finger or a pencil. When they reached the top they tried with their antennae to decide what was higher up, but before too long they just changed their tactile reactivity and walked down again, much like a ladybird which reaches the top of a child's finger then spreads its wings and flies away. Since stick insects have no wings they are presumably programmed merely to try again somewhere else. Many years ago I had some young crayfish in an aquarium in which there were also the empty shells of young water snails. One morning I observed that all the young crayfish were sitting inside these shells, their tails inside, their heads turned towards the entrance, just as hermit crabs do. This striking observation led me to consider preadaptation: how habits and anatomy change. The mental and neurological equipment of mankind, I thought, have not undergone any significant changes for a very long time, and maybe we should begin to approach the problem of the acquisition and development of new faculties from the point of view of preadaptation, a fertile way of looking at things.

I later experimented with chemotaxis in my *Paramecium* period (1938) and became interested in such areas as the behaviour of a small starfish, an organism which has five independent nerve centres at the tips of its arms, in a gravitational field and in light gradients.

During my tenure of the Animal Behaviour presidency I tried to broaden the outlook of the members by setting up joint meetings with other scientific societies, and to steer a course between the conflicting tendencies amongst the committee members.

My election as Treasurer of the Association of British Zoologists was, I am sure, *faute de mieux*, and my task indisputably was to rescue this peculiar club from financial ruin. The Association had been founded by a small group of zoologists some time after the First World War. They were all members of the Association for the Advancement of Science who donated a few hundred pounds so that they could meet once a year at Christmas time. There was no annual subscription. After the Second World War, which had interrupted those meetings, inflation ate away at the capital and I took it upon myself to locate the bank account – not easy – and to get permission from the surviving trustees to reinvest the money. I also launched two appeals for additional contributions and new members. After almost a decade the Association was disbanded, having outlived its usefulness. By then zoology was no longer a well-defined discipline but a rag-bag of loosely connected sciences.

It was when I was involved with the Association for the Advancement of Science in the first or second year of the last war that I attended a discussion on the role and behaviour of scientists in wartime. Several speakers fiercely attacked the German scientists who had jingoistically supported the Kaiser in the Great War.

Reference was made to a motion passed at the time. When a fervently patriotic resolution was passed at the end of our session I was struck by the similarity of the two declarations and became annoyed. But when I looked around me I could observe no one protesting, not even the chubby little man sitting next to me who turned out to be H. G. Wells. Arriving home and still angry, I wrote a paper entitled: 'Separation and Reintegration as phases in Evolution', including a number of deliberations which had been occupying my mind for some time. There seems to be only a tenuous connection between the cause of my anger and the subject of my paper.

Besides the societies I have already mentioned I am a founder member of the International Society for Biological Rhythms. But as a general rule I have preferred to support small groups whose survival is precarious, while the large organisations (which will easily survive without my support or approval) are dominated by people about whom I know very little, and of whom I usually disapprove.

From time to time I am sent a paper or a book for shortening, emendation, editing or review. With most of them there is no great problem; they are either acceptable or they are not. But a few are not so straightforward.

Many years ago I received for refereeing from the editors of *Nature* a reprint of a book by a venerable and highly esteemed colleague in which he claimed to have made an important discovery. There existed, he claimed, sub-types of hereditary colour-deviant vision which are very frequent and which could easily be used as marker genes in human genetical research. Naturally this had evoked considerable interest. But when I read it through I found it full of loopholes and highly improbable. None the less I had no wish to appear to be censoring an eminent man's work and suggested that although I did not agree with the paper's conclusions, it was only a short piece, and they should print it.

A week later I was contacted by the science editor of *The Times*, which produced for the general public short abstracts of the latest findings in *Nature*. Should they publish a short paragraph on this paper? They expected me to agree, but I explained that, while I was not prepared to suppress the publication or original findings by meritorious men, I ought to do what I could to prevent them making a fool of themselves in front of the public; the young editor was dissuaded from publishing his paragraph.

The Lancet publishes reviews anonymously and this can occasionally cause problems. I received from the magazine a book by a famous colleague who had strayed outside his regular disciplines and had written an exceedingly bad and, in my view, dangerous work. In my review I argued that the book deserved to be pulped and should not be released into general circulation. The editor asked me, could I not blunt a little the sharpness of my comments? Had I been required to sign my review I would have refused to countenance the emasculation of my comments in any particular. But since my piece would be anonymous I had to consider what would happen if the review was left as it was. An alternative review would be commissioned to stand beside mine, and it would almost certainly come from one of the young disciples of the great man, and would therefore be highly laudatory. Thus I agreed to soften my criticisms, and use a more conventional means of expressing them.

The task of the referee who has to judge the worth of a publication before it is accepted is hazardous indeed. I suspect that some of my most original work failed to find a publisher as a result of conventionally-minded referees.

Until 150 years ago science was principally a solitary occupation. It was the German dye and drug industries that first employed a larger collective research base. Nowadays there are branches of science in which the solitary worker cannot hope to achieve anything. Particle physics, genetic engineering, biochemistry and any kind of industrial or agricultural research require a quantity of integrated workers. But I firmly believe that there remains a place for the solitary worker; originality breeds more freely amongst the solitary, and their breakthroughs are frequently the starting point for large-scale developments. Most of my professional life I have worked on my own or with a very small number of colleagues; I have not run out of projects that can be attacked in this way.

This matter of originality is not straightforward. It was considered perfectly natural for the early classical composers to incorporate great chunks of other people's music in their concerts, since music at that time was written more for specific occasions than for posterity. What is original and what is derivative in one's own mind is not easy to disentangle. I have written long passages which I believed at the time to be original, but which turned out to be paraphrases of other sources forgotten by me at the moment of composition. Sometimes I had even plagiarised my own work. How can one therefore in science or the arts distinguish between the deliberate imitation or the self-conscious felony? I have several times noticed that I have the curious ability to imitate in my own writing, albeit unconsciously, the style of some fine work of literature or poetry after I have been reading that work.

There are two distinctions commonly made in respect of science, neither of which I could accept. Those who distinguish between basic and applied science miss the point. Those engaged in basic research can never be quite sure in what way and when their results may find an application. Conversely, the applied scientist pursuing practical goals, will often stumble over unresolved basic problems. Unless he can disentangle these himself, or have a colleague do it for him, he will have to abandon his practical work.

The other distinction which I find hard to accommodate is that between elementary and advanced work, as taught, for instance, in the lower and upper classes of middle school. Advanced work seems to imply the application of technique, borrowed from a neighbouring discipline which the beginner may not have had a chance to master.

The claim that there are more scientists alive today than have lived in the whole of history may well be true. It follows that they will differ from their predecessors. I believe them to be on the whole less original and more professional, more interested in technique than in philosophy, more used to working in groups than alone. There exists a new type of isolation; people working in the same field, even in the same institution, may not know of one another's existence. On more than one occasion while I have been abroad, I have been introduced to fellow workers from my own college of whose existence I had no inkling. The enormous accumulation of data and the rapid change of methods make many scientists of the last generation appear to be figures from the remote past. Young people who see my name quoted in this or that publication have often asked me whether 'Kalmus' was my father, perhaps, or my uncle.

This curious contraction of time may be observed elsewhere than in science. When I was naughty as a little boy in Prague, my nursemaid threatened me with the Swedes, who had overrun half

145

the town in 1648; when my young daughter heard her mother criticise a misquotation from one of Churchill's speeches, she refused to believe that we had actually heard that speech when it was first transmitted on the radio.

The impact of modern techniques has been enormous in biology. Many of the projects that had attracted me as a young man were quite impractical then, whether they related to the functioning of a single organism or the exploration of the sea-bed. How fish behave in the deepest regions of a coral reef had to be inferred in those days by putting together single observations, guessing their temporal sequence, and producing a hypothetic picture of the likely course of events. But now with diving equipment, sophisticated lighting sources and photographic equipment, one may, in a few minutes' observation, gain more insight than would have been possible in a lifetime of scholarly investigation. In fields such as physiology the old mechanical and optical methods had outlived their usefulness, and for a while the new electronic devices were little better. But now the number of observations has multiplied enormously, accuracy is vastly improved, and elaboration has been made possible, all by computer. But there remain one or two of the old techniques which have still not been fully exploited. Rather late in life I learned about using a strong lamp with a reflector attached to my forehead when walking through nocturnal tropical forests. This is an unfair and illegal tool for poachers, but invaluable for the naturalist. In a curious way it mirrors the old idea that the eyes are not the receptors but the emitters of light. The eyes of tree crabs reflect back the light. Bush-babies and lizards, owls and gazelles, medium-sized cats; there is so much more life around than one could have possibly supposed, and all of it staring at the light in fascination. The moving shadows of the walking naturalist add to the impression that here is an ambience unlike anything ever before experienced.

I have invented quite a few scientific aids in my life, but never realised their potential nor was sufficiently interested in exploiting them for profit. The plankton filter pump was one notable invention, but there were others more far-reaching. I experimented in small enclosed ambiences populated with two or three species and only receiving energy through glass walls; this ante-dated the proposed use of plant assimilation in spacecraft. I interrupted behavioural and overt psychological processes by putting organisms, insects for instance, in a vacuum, a technique now applied to operations on the human brain. Circulation is interrupted and chilling takes place as the surgery proceeds.

On a more mundane level and much to the disgust of my mother, I mixed fruit and fruit preserves with yoghurt; you can find a similar blend today on the shelf of any supermarket. It did not occur to me that I was doing anything remarkable. Surely anyone confronted with similar situations would stumble on the same conclusions.

Just before the outbreak of the Second World War I was employed in reconstituting a patent which would have made it possible to take the bitterness out of soya beans, and to purify cooking fats and oils. Wartime regulations meant that the patent could not be exploited, although I still own a bundle of shares in a company founded to do just that. Had I grown up in a different tradition I might have been more inclined to market these ideas, but, if I had done so, I could well have been deflected from my chosen route. I would, I believe, have been wealthier – and unhappier – than I am now.

Two of the richest areas in which I worked were tune deafness and colour blindness. It was with my friend, the phonetician, D. B. Fry, that I became interested in the heredity of tune deafness, also known as 'tone deafness', which shows itself most commonly in people when they try to sing. Not everybody who cannot sing in tune, however, is tune deaf, but no one who is truly tune deaf can sing in tune, nor play any instrument which requires the player to modify the pitch.

Our studies were quite leisurely, extending themselves over some 30 years. This had the advantage of enabling us to test the same people as children and as adults; we found that the condition persists. We were also able to test the ability to recognise tunes with what we called our 'distorted tunes' test. We would play a few bars of a number of well-known melodies, in which there were several wrong notes, and then ask the subject to indicate on a form which of the snippets were correctly played, and which not. Just as normally sighted people cannot conceive that the colour-blind are unable to read colour charts, so the normally musical are puzzled when others quite fail to spot the most glaring dissonants, and the most curious harmonies. After conducting so many of these tests I now find it difficult myself to identify whether or not the music is correctly played, and from this I deduce that the rules of diatonic music are acquired, and hence that one can, though not without effort, learn to appreciate contemporary music. I tested an Italian conductor who had no problems, but who was also able to tell us which modern composers would have written our distorted versions!

In cross-cultural tests we presented German melodies to English people and English melodies to German people and our results clearly indicated that people could recognise mistakes even in unfamiliar melodies, just so long as these pieces were written in the conventions of folk-song and classical music. We were never able to devise a successful tune deaf test for those unused to Western music. If they failed our original test, it did not necessarily follow that they were tune deaf. I concluded that while tune deafness is the main factor preventing people from acquiring any significant musical ability, it does not stop them enjoying music, any more than colour-blindness stops the victims enjoying great paintings.

While conducting experiments into colour-blindness, I encountered a vast pedigree of people who suffer from a specific form of optical degeneration, which leads in some three or four years to blindness. The condition is a dominant one, that is to say that on average half of the sufferer's offspring will be exposed to the danger of also becoming blind. But the condition only starts to show itself in middle age, often in the late fifties, but this is too late to be able to counsel the children whether or not they will fall victim to the condition themselves, and whether they will transmit the relevant gene to his or her offspring. In such a situation genetical advice is rather pointless. It was quite possible that colour-blindness would be a relevant factor amongst those who would succumb; but my experiments indicated that colour-blindness was entirely independent of the more serious condition and could not be used as an indicator of future pathological developments.

There was a similar situation with a middle-aged taxi-driver who came to see me accompanied by his wife. His colour vision, he said, had deteriorated recently. Was he going blind or was it natural deterioration due to advancing years? Unfortunately I had to tell him that he was a candidate for the familiar blindness and that he should look around for another job before he was completely incapacitated. I wondered whether I ought to report him to the authorities, as he already was and clearly would become a greater danger on the highways. But he followed my advice and I was spared this painful decision.

The language in which one gives genetical counselling, and the method one employs, is vital. A woman appeared in the department one day who had given birth to two children who had died at an early age from a recessive condition which suggested that any further children would have a one-quarter probability of succumbing to the same disease. One could either tell her that her chances of producing an affected child were one in four, but because she clearly was desperately keen to try again, one might do better to tell her that the chance of the child being normal was three in four and might well be taken. As it happened she had approached another member of the department as well as myself, but had told neither of us of her duplicity. Both myself and my colleague had agreed on diagnosis and prognosis, but we had given different advice.

It was in the course of my studies of hereditary differences in human sense-perception that I decided to find out whether genetical polymorphism, such as colour-blindness, tune deafness or 'taste blindness' could also be found in our nearest relations, the non-human anthropoids. I was unconvinced by previous work in this area, and welcomed any opportunities of working with chimpanzees, gorillas, orang-utans and gibbons. Fisher, Ford and Huxley published a paper in *Nature*, following the International Congress of Genetics in Edinburgh, in which they seemed to show that monkeys can indeed be classified into those who can taste low concentrations of the bitter substance, phenylthiocarbonide (PTC), and those who cannot. Moreover they suggested that the proportions were similar to those found in man. This last statement aroused my suspicions, because by 'man' the three researchers clearly meant 'white man', and they gave the ratio of tasters to non-tasters amongst 'man', as about three to one. But there are many non-tasters amongst African and Amerindian populations. Do we therefore conclude that European man is closer to the chimpanzee than the dark-skinned races?

In 1965 Dr Geoffrey H. Bourne kindly permitted me to test the apes in Orange Park, Florida, an institution famous for primate studies, now transferred to Atlanta. At first I experimented with liquids, but later had the idea of incorporating PTC into ice-cream. It worked beautifully. The chimpanzees reacted violently, some spitting it out, grimacing, and throwing tantrums, while others swallowed their ice-creams with pleasure. The gorillas were less demonstrative, either taking the food or refusing it. But the reactions of the orangs were most intriguing. Most of them spat the mixture into a hollowed hand, tasting it again and again pensively. Mood, circumstances, and habituation can greatly modify the behaviour of these animals, of course, and I felt unable to reach any very definite conclusions after such limited research, but the existence of a taste polymorphism in primates can certainly not be excluded. Better evidence was published later, according to which the polymorphism seems even to occur in laboratory mice.

Looking at my life as a whole, I am struck by two features. It is most improbable that I should have survived in such murderous times while millions, including most of my relatives and friends, perished. And, even more astonishingly, that I have been able, despite all this adversity, to follow my earliest inclinations, and to devote most of my efforts to research. Looking for a single common feature in my multifarious career, I can discover only one which is quite independent of local and temporal circumstances: playfulness.

I believe that this was first brought to my attention some 20 years ago after a seminar on colour-blindness when, in answer to the provocative question of a young student, I indulged myself in some free-wheeling speculation concerning the evolution of colour vision. Taken aback by my uninhibited exhibition of playful thinking, he asked, amidst some general embarrassment: 'Professor Kalmus, did you ever do any work?'

I think that this question was a most illuminating assessment of my personality. I have rarely done anything for any length of time that I did not like. Though doubts about the seriousness of scientific pursuits are nowadays no longer fashionable, they used to be. After I described to him my first experiments on circadian rhythms, an elderly relative asked in some bewilderment: 'Do adults really do such things?'

Today scientists are more often asked whether they have considered the serious consequences of their labours. Indeed, most scientists take their work very seriously; it is only the old ones who then write funny books on 'Scientific Method'.

I have been lucky. Only a few people are privileged to be permitted to play about successfully, and it is understandable, indeed natural, that mature scientists should encourage the young to pursue a particular circumscribed objective. An older colleague once reported to me that von Frisch considered me to be quite a talented fellow and remarked: 'If only this young man could stick to one subject.' I have never managed that. But I believe that I owe such success as my work may have enjoyed to my – the word is apt – playfulness.

11

Old Bird's Eye View

In what follows I do not intend to analyse my character, nor provide an apology for my life. I want instead to consider the effects of transplantation at the age of 33, from the collapsing liberal regime in German Prague to a London preparing for war.

In some respects the effects have been remarkably insignificant. When lecturing at a German university or when enjoying a holiday in Austria, I still feel entirely at home with the language and am seldom taken for a stranger. In contrast I have only to open my mouth in England to be recognised immediately as a foreigner; this after almost a half-century of working and teaching in Britain and some very competent instruction in phonetics. In other respects my reactions are obverse – Nussy describes them as perverse – for I feel compelled to feel and speak English when confronted with disagreeable Germans and German when in the presence of disagreeable Britishers.

Like most immigrants I have become an eclectic, taking from many influences what was most congenial. I warmed to the Englishman's concern for civil liberties, much to be preferred to the generalised feelings about liberty prevalent in my youth. But I do not accept that English law and customs are in every respect superior to Roman law and continental habits; I find the habit of English judges to abuse people in the course of conviction as abominable as the use of the cane in schools, and the role of the police in the lawcourts as absurd.

I find myself admiring Anglo-Saxon pragmatism wholeheartedly; it does not seem so very different from the Prussian virtues of duty and stolidity. But I despair of the nihilism of most contemporary English poetry, which lacks rhyme and reason, and I deplore the prevalence of satire, an art-form for the untalented and more suited to the French personality. I cannot stomach the denigration of everything German by young Germans, nor the arrogance and racism of young Israelis.

There has never been any conflict in my mind between the broad scientific attitudes, which I acquired in Prague and which I practise in England. But there is a distinction between the German and English traditions, with the American somewhere in between. The difference is one of temperament: whether to proceed methodically, deductively, step by step, under stringent critical controls, the technique which I would call the 'Cambridge approach' or the march of the infantry; or to employ the 'Freiburg approach', which allows great leaps of the imagination, unhampered by the constraints of deadening criticism, and only later checked against reality. This 'reconnaissance from the air' technique implies inductive procedure and the use of de Bono's 'lateral thinking'. It has been my observation that most scientists owe their success to a combination of the two, of straight and lateral thinking, logical discipline and a free-ranging imagination. Some are satisfied by a beautiful experiment, others by general theory. Zealots of the classical and romantic schools quarrel; some of them have merit, no doubt, but to me both factions appear to be foolish.

In most people's lives imagination provides the goal, emotion the driving force, and intelligence the means. Food, hunger and the stratagems necessary to acquire food, are connected in this way, so too are sex objects, love, and the stratagems which lead to reproduction. In the pursuit of scientific truths, these simple natural relationships are complicated, particularly in theoretical or basic research, when strong, and even obsessional, emotions may attach themselves to practical goals, that is, the means and stratagems necessary for the achievement of original and often practical goals. Scientists are not devoid of passion. But while they work their passions become engaged in the pursuit of the theoretical and the experimental towards some remote, half-forgotten end, which has long ago ceased to provide any very strong motivation.

Applying this to my own career, I can quite see that in retrospect my emotions were not sufficiently engaged in a career, in the acquisition of material goods or in sensual pleasures; I was too busy satisfying my curiosity. Compared to this powerful urge, my desire to alter the world weakened. Politics had no appeal for me; its fanatical manifestations disgusted me.

Had I listened in Renaissance Florence to the sermons of Savonarola, I would have enjoyed observing him and might even, like Leonardo, have sketched him, but I doubt that I would have been much swayed by his fulminations. I believe that this kind of detachment contributed to my escape from the Holocaust.

Detachment was also professionally useful. On several occasions disease in my family and in myself provided me with a valuable opportunity for first-hand research. Having to get up throughout the night when an infant son was ill enabled me to observe the eclosion times of *Drosophila*, which I had kept for different purposes in a cupboard in the bedroom. The apparently high incidence of various forms of cancer deaths in my family, which I unearthed when I was attempting to explore our longevity and life expectations, rather shook me at first, until I discovered that a great number of families, which had in the past been considered 'cancer families', are now considered perfectly normal. Specific cancers, like the malignancy development from dominant polyposis of the colon are a different matter.

The deterioration in my vision as a result of more than 30 bouts of corneal herpes has enabled me to study differences between my two eyes in the recovery time of light and colour perception after exposure to strong light. After reading in bed one evening I switched off the light and noticed that when I looked at a transparent curtain covering the window a sodium lamp burning nearby appeared quite yellow to my left eye, but pale and colourless to my right. The difference lasted a few minutes and then vanished. I tried several times to replicate the change from the brightly lit printed page to the dim light through the curtain, and observed the same interesting phenomenon. Later, when the streetlight had been switched off and the only illumination came from the pale moon- light I again experienced a distinction between the left and right eyes. This time the light appeared at first in the left eye and only about a minute later in the right. Clearly the two eyes differed in the speed and succession in which the cone and rod mechanisms came into operation in the process of adaptation to the dark, but it was by no means clear whether this difference was brought about by a different degree of damage to the retinae, or a stronger or less strong cloudiness in the optic media. It appeared that the latter was the case after I completed some experiments with a colleague in Heidelberg. Later, I was able to simulate my situation in normal subjects and to achieve the same result.

As a result of my own poor eyesight I had been able to make a small contribution in my specialised biological field, but it is also true that apparent disadvantages and faults play a considerable part in the various processes of evolution. For instance, in the field of colour adaptation let us assume that there is a species of predator specialising in the visual detection of one species of prey and no other. In him there might have occurred a gradual adaptation on both sides until the colour vision of the predator was perfected to spot the prey, while the prey might have perfected cryptic mimicry so as to appear inconspicuous. By sudden mutation this could not happen; the prey would be instantly spotted. So it appears that what we would normally describe as deviant and disadvantageous in the colour vision of the predator would in fact be an advantage. Many examples of this syndrome must occur in all sorts of biological contexts, though it would be difficult to prove any particular instance.

Considered in isolation, many of our organs, the eyes for example, are very faulty. So are many of our faculties, such as memory. But considered holistically many of these disadvantages can seem not just useful but necessary. The ability to be able to forget, instead of remembering everything in detail, is essential for the functioning of our memory and its effect on normal behaviour. How could one write if one could recall everything? The selection of each word would take a lifetime of sieving. Indeed, if one anticipated just how much effort would be involved in a piece of creative work and how inconvenient it might become, one might be far too daunted ever to begin.

Scientists and scholars, surveying their life's work at an advanced age, tend to be self-satisfied, defensive, or desperate. When Fellows of the Royal Society are requested to supply information for a future obituary, they are forced to be more objective, but seldom come up with anything revealing about the personality behind the papers. I prefer the obituaries written by colleagues, such as Cuvier's

155

eulogies to be found in the Proceedings of the French Academy. One of the sad consequences of getting older is the frequency with which one is asked to write the obituaries of friends. It is an interesting but sobering enterprise; to sum up a colleague's achievements is not usually too difficult, but to sum up their personality, without being superficial or cruelly derogatory is an almost hopeless task. My own view is that the most authentic presentation of one's life's work can be distilled from the critical opinions of others and from one's own introspection,

First the critics. I have already observed that my apparent eclecticism has been the cause of unfavourable comment from my colleagues. 'If only Kalmus could concentrate . . . ' They saw me as a romantic, incapable of sustained thought or detailed study. Those who observed me at seminars and during discussions were frequently affronted by the way in which I let my critical faculties reel and my imagination soar. Did I not enjoy myself too much?

During the course of my career I must have had to pass some 50 examinations, so I must have been capable of sustained discipline, sometimes at least. As Sonneborn once told me: 'If you had only stuck to Paramecium [the subject of my earliest experiments and of my first book] you would have found all the things I have discovered.' Though I was temperamentally unable to stick to any one subject for years on end, I was tenacious in a different way and would return, sometimes after several decades, to an area of research. I once started work with Dennis Fry on the inheritance of tune deafness and published a short paper on the subject, but it was 30 years before I produced the definitive research. Of course nobody could have explored the changes during childhood in tonal ability and its stability in adults without retesting the same people after long intervals. We live in an age of rapid competitive publishing and investigations of this kind are out of fashion; they do not advance one's career.

Although I enjoyed the wild free-wheeling of the imagination in my professional career, I have never been much interested in science fiction, nor indeed in any kind of fiction. Life was interesting and eventful enough as it was. Nor did speculation concerning evolution hold as much interest for me as for most Anglo-Saxon biologists. I always found how things work more intriguing than how they might have developed. Furthermore, while contemporary life may be explored experimentally, fossil life cannot.

156

As I observe my own old age I cannot fail to notice the deterioration of memory, or rather of recall. I have been interested in the processes of memory ever since, as a young man, I believed in Simon's anagram, namely static and permanent changes in some nerve cells which can be reactivated either by external events or occasionally by effort on the part of the subject. In the age of computers I have become aware that this is probably too simple an idea, and that there must be a much more dynamic concept to explain certain phenomena. Maybe one should think in terms of permanently active circuits rather than the inert form of a tape-recording.

I have experienced what everyone who grows old experiences, a deterioration of what is known as 'total' or 'instant' recall. I used always to lecture without notes, and I am pleased to have no more lectures to give, because I would almost certainly find myself routinely at a loss. If in the past I found myself at a loss I would unashamedly ask the audience for a name or a particular date, and somebody would be sure to oblige me. But there are other techniques. One is just to wait a few minutes without stress and the missing information may spontaneously emerge. Another is to run through the alphabet until I find what I am looking for. I have noticed that an obstacle to recall frequently arises. I become fixated on some erroneous word which refuses to be obliterated. But despite this I have become convinced that the forming of memories and their recall are distinct and independent processes and that in the normal way of things very little is actually forgotten; which is why so much can be recollected under hypnosis.

Like most ageing people and certainly most scientists in these fast-moving times I sometimes feel that events, techniques and even concepts have overtaken me and that I might be well advised to stop my active participation in research and exposition and become a little more modest and private. But temperamentally this would not suit me; nor could I justify it. I remember a little-known poem about a rusted, old clock in Prague, which always showed the same time. The poet charmingly points out that twice a day time creeps past the clock and it shows the same time as all the other clocks in Prague – the correct time. I believe that as we get older much which has been submerged becomes mysteriously interesting and promising once more. In the arts there is a cyclical tendency that after new

movements have become over-elaborate and have exhausted themselves, the greatest artists in the movement revert to a more
primitive style, which in their hands is shown not to be obsolete at
all, but to be capable of great new developments. I have also
observed that the most fundamental scientific and metaphysical
questions are never entirely resolved. In all universities it is
popularly taught that Pasteur proved that one cannot produce
organisms from inanimate matter. He proved no such thing, of
course; only that he himself could not find a proof, and that the ways
in which other scientists had presumed to have proved it were
incorrect. More seriously those who teach their pupils this erroneous supposition must believe that life originated from inanimate
matter, and come up with intricate theories of how this might have
been. The damage is unlimited.

There is no doubt that the study of religion and metaphysics are
closely related to thoughts about death. Doctors and priests are
familiar with the varieties of reaction to dying and death amongst
those they minister to; I would just mention two cases in which the
response to a conviction of impermanence seemed extreme.

There is a biologist and a Fellow of the Royal Society with whom I
have been loosely associated for many decades. After he retired I
noticed that he seemed to be brooding and depressed. We talked
and he confessed that, having found the arguments of some of the
more extreme evolutionists bizarre, outrageous and unconvincing,
he had reverted to the simple Christianity of his childhood, and that
he had found in that religion answers to metaphysical questions that
were far more satisfactory than some of the axiomatic systems of
theoretical evolution. I experienced an equally extreme and entirely
contradictory reaction recently. Returning from a trip abroad I
found that my secretary had left on my desk a note concerning a
telephone call from a Mr M., who was urgently requiring to know
whether humanity was about to split into two species. More
information was contained in a letter from Mr M. which was
swamped amongst my accumulated mail. He was a retired doctor,
aged 92, who was clearly much exercised about the future of
humanity, and had transferred his anxiety about his own impermanence to the durability of mankind in general. He gave no
indication of precisely how this split might occur. In my answer I
assured him that there was absolutely no evidence that this might be

taking place; on the contrary, I added, the barriers between previously unreconciled groups seemed to be breaking down.

My own preoccupation with mortality has taken some curious forms. The first loss which I suffered was the sudden death of my canary when I was just four years old. I found this most beloved of birds lying on its back one morning with its legs pathetically in the air. I had seen nothing amiss the previous day. The bird was given a post-mortem by a famous pathologist, a friend of my father, who pronounced that it had died of some liver ailment. I mourned my canary for several weeks.

Next to die was my teacher from the primary school whom we all loved very much. He died when I was in the third form. We were told that he had got up too early after an operation, that his wounds had opened and that he had died by bleeding to death. True or not, this story made a fearful impression upon me, and I dreamt about it for several nights.

During the First World War, of course, I heard of the deaths of friends of the family and distant relations. They meant little to me. But shortly after the war a much beloved aunt died after breaking her femur and being kept in a home for the aged. I was much affected by this and I conceived a notion of keeping her alive by having a part of her heart muscle cultured. I could think of no other way of ensuring some sort of immortality for someone I loved so much.

As a zoologist, I came across the work of Jennings, an American protozoologist, who worked on the immortality of the protozoa and had cultured paramecium for hundreds of generations. This was how my interest in the infusorium, to which I devoted my first book, developed.

The definition of death connects naturally with the idea of an individual, and even more specifically with the idea of a corpse. In the criminal law of some countries a murder cannot be proved unless there is a corpse; death is not demonstrable without a corpse being demonstrable. What I only came to realise later was that within certain structures inside the parameciums the micronucleus dies from time to time and has to be rejuvenated by division from the nuclei, from which I conclude that the nuclei, or rather the chromosomes within them, are the potentially immortal structures of life.

My own life has frequently been put at risk. On several occasions while mountaineering I fell from rock-faces but was caught on the rope. More than once I was threatened by avalanches. Once when I was holidaying in the Alps I received an urgent request to return to Prague. It was a time of massive blizzards, and I had to traverse, together with a friend, a narrow valley with gulleys on either side, and down through these fissures came the avalanches. We climbed over them as best we could, and I arrived at the railway station in time.

In later years, with a wife and family, I became more cautious. But I still skied and, when Nussy sometimes objected to my adventures, I pointed out to her that I was far more likely to fall victim to the North London traffic on the way to and from college every day than on those few occasions when I went climbing or skiing.

I think I have always been quite conscious that the spell of my life is limited and that it is unreasonable to embark on projects the completion of which would take too many years, unless I feel that there are others who might complete them on my behalf. In most everyday decisions, though, I proceed as if my death were highly unlikely. The prevailing attitude today can best be summarised by a saying of Lucretius, which, roughly translated, reads as follows: 'Where there is death, I am not. Where I am there is no death.' But all this attitude does is to sweep the problem under the carpet, permitting no great metaphysical thoughts at all. The situation would then be that one is not afraid of death but possibly afraid of some peculiar, disagreeable method of dying; a prolonged period of suffering for oneself and those near to one. There is more to the common attitude to death than merely this. There may be frustration that all life's efforts have been in vain, and that so much that needs to be done will now never get done. There may be a sense of liberation if the processes of ageing have become too painful or undignified. But in any case there is not a proper subject for scientific speculation, which cannot deal in metaphysics. As soon as one accepts a belief in miracles or transfiguration or an afterlife, then one moves into the realms of fantasy. There is no reason why one should not do this, but it is not scientific.

Death is a precondition for ensuring someone's importance but death is only a necessary cause for such a judgement, not a sufficient cause. I am well aware that I may turn out to have been quite unimportant – even uninteresting; yet may I be excused for hoping otherwise?

The end of an autobiography is traditionally reserved for some kind of summary of the philosophy of the man's life. The story itself may have been clouded by forgetfulness and invaded by sentimentality, yet, in the case of creative people, it usually represents an attempt to demonstrate some clear line and purposeful development. I feel a long way removed from all this. Most of the problems which confronted me during my lifetime still remain unresolved.

I have never been much bothered about religion. My schools instructed me in the Protestant, Catholic and Jewish faiths, and that threefold education taught me tolerance. But I have been an agnostic since I can remember. My training in palaeontology made it impossible for me to accept any fundamentalist beliefs in the literal truth of the Genesis stories, while the accepted version of Christ's Resurrection struck me as a muddle. Either you were dead or you were not. Resurrection clearly indicated that you had not been dead. I have studied cryptobiosis, and experimented with the revival of animals (African dipterous larvae) which had for many years been in a dormant desiccated state. And I have more than once been resuscitated myself.

I was not concerned with the idea of the supernatural. Anything that happened was, by definition, 'natural'. Miracles could not be intellectually acceptable. As a child there was much that I could not understand – indeed there still is – but to explain them by an *ad hoc* suspension of the normal rules seems to me wholly unsatisfactory. Mysticism I found intolerable. The experience of Holy Communion, during which I was overcome by vague but cosmic feelings, seemed to me an hour later detestable, unrepeatable. However, the text from St Matthew given to me while I took the Host was very appropriate for my entire career: 'Ask, and it shall be given you; seek, and ye shall find; knock, and it shall be opened unto you.'

Having never been deeply immersed in fundamentalism, or doctrinal matters, I was spared the traumas of liberating myself from them, and could turn my attention to contemplating the arguments against religion. Many of these were as arbitrary and ill-founded as the orthodox arguments, and some were clearly misleading, such as the grotesque attempts to deduce ethics from the Second Law of Thermodynamics, the willingness of modern psychology to operate

161

without some unifying idea such as a 'soul', and psychoanalysts' reification of the different levels of the psyche. My juvenile and impatient agnosticism has matured into a more sedate form. I believe in most of the common values of the great religions, and in religion without revelation, as proposed by Huxley.

Most of my life has been spent researching processes and life cycles as they affect an individual life, or many generations of lives. This may not have been the most useful way to channel my energies. But thinking introspectively, I have discerned *something* which could perhaps be defined as the invariable constant characteristics of a personality, and the consciousness of being that personality. Nor does it invalidate this discernment when facts of time and circumstances are thrown at the concept. My training in rational procedures has brought me to accept Descartes' dictum: *Cogito, ergo sum,* even to wish that it were extended to accommodate a much wider meaning. Doubts about my own existence have never assailed me nor have I had any quandary concerning my identity or properties, no matter how fashionable such a crisis may have become. But I have no very clear ideas about the nature and extent of this identity of mine, nor any fixed notion as to what may happen to it.

Index

Index

Rutherford, Lord (Ernest), 21

St Albans, 105
Salisbury (painter), 73
São Paulo (University), 114
Savonarola, Girolamo, 154
Schoenberg, Arnold, 2
Schopenhauer, Arthur, 51
Schwartz, Dr, 42, 43
Schweitzer, Albert, 71
Shakespeare, William, 50
Simpson, Esther, 50
Sitte, Kurt, 102
Skoplje, 43, 44, 45
Sonneborn, Tracy, 91, 98, 99, 156
Southampton, 93
Spinoza, Benedict, 109, 110
Spurway, Helen, 56, 58, 59, 60, 61, 69, 80, 81, 131, 132
Stalin, Joseph, 63, 64
Sterne, Laurence, ix
Sturm, Professor, 13
Szolnok, 29

Tagore, Rabindranath, 125, 130
Tattersfield, Dr Frederic, 74, 75
Teissier (biologist), 74
Terrasopolis, 115

Thorn, Mr (Society for Protection of Science and Learning), 50
Tintagel, 106
Toronto, 92
Trieste, 39
Trivandrum (Zoological Institute), 129

Uraniborg, 128

Varanasi (University), 129–30
Varna (research institute), 41, 42
Vavilov (geneticist), 63
Vienna, 2, 26, 29, 33, 46, 77, 108
Villefranche-sur-Mer, 41, 42
Voltaire, 110

Wagner, Richard, 2, 87
Watson, Professor D. M. S., 51, 52, 56, 88
Weber, Carl Maria von, 2
Weiss, Paul, 42
Wells: G. P., 51, 92; H. G., 51, 143
Wiener, Norbert, 104, 105
Williams, C. B., 72
Wolf, Pastor, 20
Woolf, Virginia, 59

Zemlinski, Alexander von, 27